TABLE OF CONTENTS

GLOSSARY

Abiogenesis	The idea that life can spontaneously generate from non-life
Analogy	Correspondence in function or position between organs of dissimilar evolutionary origin or structure
Biogenesis	The idea that life can only come from life
Biogenetic Law	The theory that the stages in an organism's embryonic development and differentiation correspond to the stages of evolutionary development characteristic of the species
Carnivore	A flesh-eating animal
Cosmology	The quantitative (usually mathematical) study of the universe in its totality and humanity's place in it
Curator	The person in charge of a museum
Cynodont	small carnivorous reptiles
DNA	Deoxyribonucleic acid. A nucleic acid molecule that contains the genetic instructions used in the development and functioning of all living organisms
Echolocation	A process of using sound waves and their reflection to locate objects
Ecosystem	An ecological community together with its environment, functioning as a unit
Endosymbiosis	The condition in which one of two dissimilar organisms lives inside the other
Epidermis	The outermost living layer of an animal
Estuary	The wide part of a river near the sea where fresh and salt water mix
Genome	a full set of chromosomes; all the inheritable traits of an organism
Habitat	The area or environment where an organism or ecological community normally lives
Homology	a fundamental similarity based on common descent
Ichthyology	That branch of zoology dealing with fishes
Invertebrate	A creature that does not have a backbone

Inside the London Natural History Museum.

Kind	The original organisms (and their descendants) created supernaturally by God as described in Genesis 1 that reproduce only members of their own kind within the limits of pre-programmed information, but with great variation
Mammal	Any of various warm-blooded vertebrate animals characterized by a covering of hair on the skin and, in the female, milk-producing mammary glands for nourishing the young
Marine	Native to or inhabiting the sea
Marsupial	Mammals in which the female typically has a pouch in which it rears its young through early infancy
Materialism	The system of thought holding that the material world is all that there is
Monotreme	An order of egg-laying mammals restricted to Australia and New Guinea and consisting of only the platypus and the echidna
Naturalism	The system of thought holding that all phenomena can be explained in terms of natural causes and laws without recourse to spiritual or supernatural explanations
Organelle	A specialized part of a cell having some specific function
Ornithologist	A person who studies birds
Placental	Mammals having a placenta—an organ that nourishes the developing young by receiving nutrients from the mother's blood and passing out waste
Placoderms	Any of various extinct fishes, characterized by bony plates of armor covering the head and flanks, hinged jaws, and paired fins
Postcranial	Consisting of parts or structures behind the cranium
Symbiosis	A close interaction between creatures of two different species
Tetrapod	any vertebrate having four limbs
Theropod	Any of various large carnivorous saurischian dinosaurs of the suborder Theropoda, characterized by bipedal locomotion, large jaws, and short forelimbs
Unconformity	a discontinuity in rock sequence indicating interruption of sedimentation, commonly accompanied by erosion of rocks below the break
Venomous	Having a gland or glands for secreting venom; able to inflict a poisoned bite, sting, or wound
Vertebrate	A creature that has a backbone

SECTION I
BEFORE YOU GO

Museums are found the world over—from one-room exhibits filled with local fossils to grandiose halls loaded with specimens from every part of the globe. For most people, natural history museums conjure up images of stuffy rooms filled with evidence of life from ages past: fossils of dinosaurs, chunks of rock, chips of meteorites, tools of ancient man. Although each is unique in presentation, every museum (with few exceptions) is united around a common goal: to tell the history of the universe from a naturalistic point of view. This view, by definition, excludes any type of supernatural intervention or revelation, and attempts to explain how things made themselves. "Evolution" and "millions of years" stories abound throughout their presentations.

Is it possible for a Bible-believing Christian to visit such a place and yet leave with his faith intact? As we'll see, the answer is a resounding "yes!" Yes, we *can* learn about the natural world, and we *can* do it from a biblical perspective.

Before you go, you'll want to learn how to tell what is true from what is fiction by learning to be discerning, as the Bible exhorts us to be (Proverbs 2:1-5, Philippians 1:9, Hebrews 5:14). We need to become like the Christians in Berea, who examined the Scriptures to see if what they were being taught was true (Acts 17:10-12).

We can do this by understanding the nature of science and biblical history.

Operational science conducts experiments in the present. Origins science uncovers what happened in the past.

WHAT IS SCIENCE?

The kind of science that we normally think of as science (called "operational science") is a wonderful tool that helps researchers discover new vaccines, find new kinds of fish in previously-uncharted waters, build more fuel-efficient cars, chart a course to other planets, and devise new treatments for old diseases. With this kind of science, people can uncover fossils or study the composition of rocks.

However, operational science has limitations. It can't, for example, tell us where fish came from, when the rock formed in the first place, or how the bones of the creature came to be fossilized. Operational science deals with the world of today. It involves testing and repeating experiments.

Origins science deals with the past. Origins or historical science is used to reconstruct events that have happened in the past, using principles such as causality (for every effect, there must be a cause) and analogy (if this is the way it happens today, then perhaps it happened like this in the past). Of course, the best method of reconstruction is to rely on the account of an accurate eyewitness.

Naturalists have no such eyewitness to rely on. However, the Bible provides a written record of an eyewitness to (who was also intimately involved in) history—the Creator God. This eyewitness cannot lie, so His account is completely trustworthy. We can use this written record as our foundation for understanding the world around us. This will help us to understand why the world is the way it is today and to make sense of where we came from and why we're here.

As you go through the museum, be sure to look for statements which fall under operational science—e.g., "this fossil was found in Montana"—and statements which fall under origins science—e.g., "this fossil is 65 million years old."

God's original creation was a beautiful, "very good" place.

II

OVERVIEW OF BIBLICAL HISTORY

Creation

In Genesis 1 God reveals to us how and when He created everything. He created the animals, the stars, the moon, and man by speaking them into existence. On Day 1 God created the earth, space, time, and light. On Day 2 He separated the waters on and above the earth. On Day 3 He created dry land and all the kinds of plants and trees. On Day 4 God created the sun, moon, and stars. On Day 5 He created the many sea and flying kinds. Day 6 was when God created the land animal kinds and man.

When God created the first man and woman, He made them different from the animals (1 Corinthians 15:39). He created Adam out of the dust of the ground and Eve out of Adam's rib. God created man and woman in His image (Genesis 1:26–27). They were able to fellowship with their Creator God. When we carefully study the Bible, we learn that God took six days close to 6,000 years ago to create all the original kinds of plants and animals, the whole universe—the sun, moon, and stars—and Adam and Eve. Everything was perfect, and God called all He had created "very good" (Genesis 1:31, Deuteronomy 32:4).

Now, the animals that we see in museums do not look exactly like the animal kinds that God originally created on Days 5 and 6. Why? Glad you asked!

Animal Kinds and Adaptations
On Day 3, God created the various plant *kinds*, and on Days 5 and 6 He created the various animal *kinds*. What is an animal (or plant) "kind"? Most likely, a kind represents a group of animals that can mate with others in that group. It is not necessarily the same grouping as the "species" designation that we use today.

For example, lions, tigers, jaguars, and leopards are classified as different species, but are probably all members of an original cat kind. And donkeys, zebras, Thoroughbreds, and Arabians are probably all part of one of the original horse kinds. Some have suggested that there may have been as many as 50 different dinosaur kinds. For example, the ceratopsian kind might include triceratops, monoceratops, etc.

What did these original kinds look like? We don't know for sure. But the representatives of each kind that survived the Flood had enough information in their DNA to produce the wide variety of animals that we see today. (DNA is the molecule inside the body's cells that stores the genetic information that determines the growth and development of that organism.) For more information on the original kinds, see www.answersingenesis.org/go/kinds.

Stewardship

After God created Adam and Eve, He told them to be fruitful and multiply (Genesis 1:28) and to have dominion over the creation (Genesis 1:26, 28). They were to tend the garden and to eat from its produce. They were also to care for the animals. God owns the earth (Psalm 24:1), but He has asked us to be responsible stewards of His creation (which is now suffering from the Curse). We can do this in many ways (for example, by not littering or polluting our air or water unnecessarily). Stewardship can be taken to an extreme by placing the animals over humans, but we need to be careful to avoid this mentality. Man is God's special creation, since we were created in God's image (Genesis 1:26–27). Let's all do our part to be good stewards of the world that God gave us so that others can also enjoy it.

Corruption (The Fall)

God's creation was perfect; there was no sickness, pain, or death. But this perfect creation did not last long. God placed Adam and Eve in the Garden of Eden where they could enjoy His creation. God gave Adam and Eve a rule: don't eat of the Tree of the Knowledge of Good and Evil. God told them that if they ate of it, they would die. One day Eve was walking in the Garden, and a serpent spoke to her. He questioned God's goodness to Eve, and he tempted her to eat the fruit from the Tree of the Knowledge of Good and Evil. Eve ate of the fruit and disobeyed God. She then gave the fruit to Adam, and he ate. This disobedience was sin against a holy God. And since God is completely holy (without sin), He had to punish that sin. God had warned Adam and Eve that if they ate of the Tree, they would die. When God came to walk with them that evening, He punished their sin. The earth was now cursed. Death was now part of life; both animals and humans would now die (Genesis 3:19; Romans 8:20–22). When the first humans sinned, it corrupted all of creation. The ground was cursed and would produce thistles and thorns (Genesis 3:17–18). Animals began to hunt and eat other animals. Man would now have to work hard for food, and woman would have pain in bearing and raising her children (Genesis 3:16–17). From this time on, each person would be born with a sin nature, and we all reject God. Adam and Eve's first sin is called "the Fall."

Death

Since death was a result of the Fall, you may wonder what Adam, Eve, and the animals ate in the very beginning, right after they were created. According to God's Word, they ate plants (Genesis 1:29–30). Even though this answer sounds simple, it has caused some to wonder about the difference between plant life and animal and human life. Death was a result of the Fall, but if plants died before the Fall, then death was present before sin. According to the Word of God, there is a difference between plant life and animal and human life. Throughout the Bible, the Hebrew words *nephesh chayyâh* are used to describe human and animal life. When referring to mankind, *nephesh chayyâh* means "living soul" or "soulish creature," and when it refers to animals, it means "living creature." However, this word is never applied to plant life. There is a plain distinction. It is easy to see that plants do not experience pain, suffering, or death in the same way that humans and animals do. Their death is not the death of a "living soul" or "living creature."

Included with plants are possibly invertebrates, since they too were excluded from the *nephesh chayyâh* creatures. To gain a better understanding that there was no living-creature death before the Fall of Adam, we must correctly read what God has written. God's Word plainly teaches that death is the result of sin. Therefore, there was no human or animal (*nephesh chayyâh*) death before sin. Adam, Eve, and all the animals ate plants before the Fall.

Defense-Attack Structures

The Bible tells us that before the Fall, every animal ate only plants and vegetables (Genesis 1:29–30). Death (human, as well as animal death) entered the world as a result of Adam's sin (Romans 5:12; 8:20–22). It was only after the Flood that God gave man permission to eat other things besides plants (Genesis 9:3). As you look at the animals in the museum, you may wonder how there could be no animal death before Adam sinned, when so many animals look like they were designed to attack and eat other animals, or to defend themselves from other animals. There are several possible explanations.

First, the harmful structures (like sharp teeth, poison, and claws) may have been used for different functions before the Fall, and animals only began using them for attack and defense afterward. A second possibility is that the animals may have been redesigned after the Fall, as part of God's curse on all of creation, including the animals (remember, the form of the serpent was changed—Genesis 3:14). And finally, it is also possible that since God foreknew the Fall would happen, He could have "programmed" the information for these structures in the first animals, and "switched it on" after the Fall.

The most important thing to remember about defense and attack structures is that they were *not* part of God's original creation, as such. They are a result of the Curse on creation after Adam sinned.

Catastrophe (The Flood)

The sons and daughters of Adam and Eve continued to turn their backs on their Creator and do their own thing. Their children and grandchildren were so wicked that God decided to judge the earth and everything that lived on the earth. But God knew one man who followed Him. That man was Noah. God spoke with Noah and told him that He was going to judge the earth by water—a global flood. However, God had chosen to spare Noah. So He told Noah to build an Ark, which would hold his wife, his sons, their wives, and two of every kind of air-breathing, land animal and bird (and seven of some). This boat was huge. It was approximately 450 feet (135 meters) long and 45 feet (13.5 meters) tall.

It took Noah quite a while to build his boat (probably around 70 years), but once he, his family, and the animals were on board, God closed the door. Then for 40 days and nights, the water in the atmosphere (rain) fell. The fountains of the great deep (waters in the earth) broke open. For 150 days, water flooded the whole earth, covering even the earth's highest hills by over 22 feet (7 meters). And the waters remained on the earth for many more months.

Finally, just over a year after the Flood started, Noah and his family could leave the Ark. All the people and land animals outside the Ark died. The waters were so powerful that tons of rocks and dirt were moved around during the Flood. Plants, animals, and even humans became buried in the muddy sediments. The remains of some of these have been dug up today; they are called fossils. Not all fossils are from the Flood, but most of them are. After the floodwaters drained into the ocean basins, the whole earth was changed—mountains, valleys, canyons, the climate ... everything. This happened around 4,300 years ago—approximately 2348 BC.

Extinction

When all members of a certain type of animal die out, that animal is said to have gone extinct. Extinction may occur because of sickness, disease, starvation, changes in habitat, or by hunting. Many animals have become extinct in the past, and extinction can happen to any animal population. One of the more famous extinct animal groups is the dinosaur. When talking about the dinosaurs, or any other extinct animal, we must keep some things in mind. First, we know that dinosaurs were real because the Bible says that land animals were created on Day 6, and since dinosaurs are land animals, they were included in this creation (sea and flying reptiles such as pteranodons and plesiosaurs were created on Day 5). We also know that dinosaurs were real because their bones have been discovered and preserved for us to see.

Second, we must remember that when God sent the Flood to punish mankind's wickedness, God preserved His creation by sending animals onto the Ark. The various kinds of dinosaurs would have also been on the Ark and preserved from the Flood. Dinosaurs could have fit on the Ark, since they were, on average, about the size of a small pony. And God would have preserved the younger representatives of the different dinosaur kinds to reproduce after the Flood.

Third, since representatives of the dinosaur kinds were on the Ark and survived the Flood, something had to have happened to them after that, which caused them to die out. There are many things that could have contributed to the extinction of the dinosaurs, including climate change, starvation, diseases, and hunting by humans and/or other animals (some of the same reasons animals today become extinct!).

Finally, we should remember that some animals that were thought to have been extinct for a long time have actually been found alive and well in different parts of the world (e.g., the coelacanth). So, is it possible to ever find a live dinosaur on earth again? Maybe ...!

The Ice Age

At the beginning of the Flood, the "fountains of the great deep" broke open, and warm water from inside the earth poured into the oceans. Eventually, the floodwaters covered the land. At the end of the Flood, the waters drained off the land into the oceans. They were still warmer than they are today from all the volcanic activity caused by the "fountains" breaking open and the land masses moving around. Being warmer, the ocean water would have evaporated much faster than it does today. Clouds formed and moved over the landmasses. But these clouds were bigger, carrying more water than today's clouds, because there was more evaporation from the oceans. So, there would have been much more snow and rain in the years after the Flood.

Also, the snow fell over a much larger area—in places that do not have snow today. That is because the volcanoes had blasted so much fine dust high into the air that the sun's warmth was blocked from the earth. So places which are warm today were much cooler then. With all the volcanic dust and clouds keeping the land cool, the snow on the ground would not have melted during the summer. Instead, it turned to ice, and gradually built up thick ice sheets which eventually covered about one-third of the land on the earth. After many years, the oceans cooled down. So with less evaporation, there was less snowfall. Also the volcanoes weren't as active and the dust cleared away, letting the sun's warmth through to melt the snow and ice each summer. Eventually the Ice Age was over. This Ice Age probably lasted around 700 years. Some scientists suggest that it peaked around 500 years after the Flood, and lasted 200 more years. (For more information, see Oard, M., *Frozen in Time*, Master Books, 2004.) From observations of today's glaciers (found on mountain tops around the world), scientists can learn how ice sheets in the past may have changed the earth's surface.

1. The ice carved away some of the rock layers laid down during the Flood, leaving behind u-shaped valleys.
2. The glaciers picked up rocks as they moved along, and the rocks scratched the underlying ones, leaving behind grooves (called striations).
3. The ice sheets crushed the rocks they gathered and, after they melted, left behind fields filled with the crushed rocks and boulders.

Although museums may claim that there have been many "ice ages" over millions of years, the truth is that there really was only one—it was one of the results of the Flood, and its effects can still be seen today!

Confusion (Tower of Babel)

Noah's descendants disobeyed the Creator's command to spread out and fill the earth after the great Flood. They wanted to stay together and began to build a tall tower (Genesis 10, 11). So, God gave to each family group a different language. This made it difficult for the groups to understand each other, and so they split apart. Each extended family went its own way, and found a different place to live. Some of the families used the land bridges that were exposed during the Ice Age to travel to different continents. Others sailed to different parts of the world. As they went, each of these groups took with it its own special set of characteristics (for instance, for lighter skin and eye color, or for darker skin and eye color). These characteristics were passed through their DNA to their children, and so on. Because the groups no longer freely mixed with other groups, the characteristics of each became more and more prominent as new generations of children were born. Eventually, the many different people groups developed.

The Good News

When Adam sinned, all of creation was cursed (Genesis 3; Romans 8:20–21). Part of that curse on man was separation between God and man. Before the Fall, Adam and Eve had walked with God in perfect fellowship, but after the Fall, sin separated man from his Creator.

Sin continues to separate us from God. God is perfect and requires those who come to live with Him to also be perfect. But we are born with a sin nature, and because we sin against God daily, we can never get to Heaven by anything that we do. God must punish sin as He punished Adam and Eve's sin in the Garden.

Our punishment is an eternity separated from God in a place commonly called "hell." It sounds hopeless, unless there is someone who would be willing to pay our sin penalty for us. That someone must be without sin (perfect). Jesus, the Son of God, is that perfect God-man who took upon Himself the penalty for our sin.

Jesus died on a cross, paying for sin; and three days later He rose again, defeating death to provide us with a way to one day live with Him. But for us to be acceptable to God, we must repent of our sins and place our faith in Jesus. We must believe that Jesus took our place on the Cross and died for us.

Even though some people say that there are many ways to God, there is actually only one way. Jesus said in John 14:6, "I am the way, the truth and the life. No one comes to the Father except through me." Jesus is our only way to be reconciled with God. We can never earn eternal life on our own, because of our sin. Jesus paid the penalty and made a way for His children to live with Him forever. We must repent of our sin and place our trust in Him—that is the good news.

Bacteria-to-butterfly evolution isn't supported by observational science.

OVERVIEW OF NATURAL HISTORY

A Big Bang

The most popular naturalistic explanation about the origin of the universe is the big bang hypothesis. At its simplest, this view suggests that the universe emerged rapidly from a hot, dense state several billions of years ago. However, there are several differing versions of the big bang idea, with disagreement among the versions. As one scientist has pointed out, there are many problems with this view.

> Big bang cosmology is probably as widely believed as has been any theory of the universe in the history of Western civilization. It rests, however, on many untested, and in some cases untestable, assumptions. Indeed, big bang cosmology has become a bandwagon of thought that reflects faith as much as objective truth. (G. Burbidge, "Why only one big bang?" *Scientific American* 266:2, 1992, p. 96.)

Eventually, according to the naturalistic worldview, our solar system originated from a spinning cloud of gas (this idea is known as the "nebular hypothesis"). As with the big bang idea, the nebular hypothesis has many scientific problems and runs counter to the biblical teaching.

For more information, visit www.answersingenesis.org/go/astronomy.

Molecules-to-Man Evolution

Over 1 billion years after the earth formed, life began from non-living matter. A popular belief today is that all animals and humans evolved (changed) from one kind into another kind over millions of years. Molecules-to-man evolution claims that everything we see happened by purely natural processes. (Some believe that in the beginning God created simple life forms, and then let natural processes take over, so that what we see today evolved from these early simple life forms. Some say that there is no God who created or began anything.)

These people would say that everything is the result of time and natural processes, that everything happened by accident. Fish-to-philosopher evolution often includes the belief that life formed from something that was not living, and then that life evolved, over millions of years, into the different animals we have today.

Some evolutionists even believe that humans evolved from apelike creatures and that dinosaurs evolved into birds. Scientists have demonstrated for us that these things are just not possible: life has never been observed to come from non-living chemicals. Animals don't change into other kinds of animals. Even though amoeba-to-architect evolution is taught in most museums (and other places), molecules-to-man evolution is not fact. It is based on the ideas of man, not on the Bible, which comes from God.

Particles-to-people evolution is taught nowhere in the Bible, and is not supported by science. Instead, from the Bible, we learn that God created plants, animals, and humans to produce "after their kind" (Genesis 1). For more information, see page 11.

Natural Selection=Evolution?

You may encounter many examples of "natural selection in action" while visiting the museum. Many evolutionists claim that natural selection is the process that drives fish-to-philosopher evolution. Amoeba-to-architect evolution requires that, over time, living things must add more information to their DNA as they gain new features, abilities, or structures. However, natural selection actually works in the *opposite* direction of what molecules-to-man evolution requires. It selects from *already-existing* genetic information, and cannot generate *new* genetic information.

God created the original animal kinds with much diversity in their DNA, so that as they reproduced and filled the earth, their descendants were able to adapt to many different environments. Scientists *have* observed this—animals reproduce "after their kind" (dogs have puppies, cats have kittens, geese have goslings, kangaroos have joeys, etc.). The genetic makeup of some members of a kind is more suitable to certain environments. Natural selection is the process by which animals die out when they don't have the genetic makeup that allows them to survive in their environment.

Those animals that survive reproduce more animals like themselves. For example, many animals that live in drier regions of the world are able to gain most of the water they need from the plants they eat. Animals without this ability would have a harder time trying to survive in that region, and would eventually die out. Natural selection is not a process that changes molecules into men over millions of years. Natural selection may bring about a new *species* of animal, but it cannot generate a new *kind* of animal.

For more information, visit www.answersingenesis.org/go/selection.

Those Millions of Years

According to naturalism, the earth and universe are several billion years old. However, the methods used to arrive at these long ages (including radioisotopes and erosion and deposition rates) are based on many assumptions. When these assumptions are taken into consideration, the results of the dating methods yield ages far more consistent with a biblical timeframe. Remember, you're not denying operational science when you deny the millions-of-years idea; you're denying a naturalistic interpretation of the past.

To find out more about the problems with the various dating methods, visit www.answersingenesis.org/go/young and www.answersingenesis.org/go/dating.

Additionally, the idea of a millions-of-years old earth is a relatively recent invention. Until the late nineteenth century, few people believed the earth to be so old. Several scriptural geologists challenged those who held to an ancient earth. For more information, see www.answersingenesis.org/go/scriptural-geologists.

Use your time at natural history museums to teach your children how to critique other views of history from a biblical perspective.

PRACTICALLY SPEAKING

What do you want to learn about?

Most large museums are filled with a wide range of exhibits. It may be helpful to narrow down what you want to learn about, and spend your time in one or two exhibit areas. Visit the museum's web page to find out what exhibits the museum offers and plan your visit accordingly.

Educational guides

Some museums provide educational guides for specific exhibits, with pre- and post-visit activity suggestions to help you get the most out of your experience. Check the website of the museum you're visiting to find out what it offers. Although these guides are written from a naturalistic perspective, they can still provide helpful information about operational science findings.

Questions to ask yourself

As you meander through the halls of learning, it may be helpful to keep in mind some questions to ask yourself, or your guide (in a polite manner with great gentleness and respect).

- How do I (you) know that to be true?
- What assumptions are being made?
- What philosophy is the conclusions based on?
- What was actually found?
- Which aspects are operational science and which are origins science?
- What is the biblical interpretation?
- Where would this fit in biblical history?

We needn't be afraid to visit natural history museums. Instead, we can use them as opportunities to learn the alternate view of history, and to critique it from a biblical perspective. Enjoy the process of learning to think biblically, and be discerning about what you see and hear. Rest in the fact that God's Word remains unchanged, while much of the museum signage will be out of date next year!

Inside the London Natural History Museum.

SECTION 2

WHILE YOU ARE THERE

This section of the guide will walk you through the major museum "halls."

Life abounds on the planet we call home. The Bible helps us understand where it all came from!

HALL OF LIFE

From the deepest depths of the ocean to the upper layers of the atmosphere, life abounds on our planet. Did life originate in the oceans? Do all living things share a common ancestor? Why is there so much amazing diversity among life forms, coupled with so much similarity? Are there really evolutionary "transitional forms"?

This section of the guide explores the answers to the questions that are raised in museum exhibits that deal with life on earth.

Can a naturalistic view of the past really explain the complexity of life today?

ORIGINS OF LIFE EXHIBITS

Molecules-to-meerkats evolution isn't supported by science. Life can only come from life!

LIFE FROM NON-LIFE

The naturalistic worldview claims that life arose from non-living chemicals. However, from the Bible, we know that God is the giver of all life. He supernaturally created the original plant kinds on Day 3, the original sea and flying kinds on Day 5, and the original land animal kinds and people on Day 6. Since He finished His supernatural creative acts at the end of the sixth day, we would not expect to see life being created out of nothing today.

The idea that life can spontaneously generate from non-life goes back at least as far as the philosophers of ancient Greece.

In the nineteenth century, creation scientist Louis Pasteur (1822–1895) performed experiments which demonstrated conclusively that "spontaneous generation" (or abiogenesis) was a fallacious idea. He showed that life can only come from life (biogenesis). Despite the scientific evidence, those who accept the naturalistic worldview (evolution) continue to accept by blind faith that long ago, non-living chemicals turned into life.

For more information, see www.answersingenesis.org/creation/v23/i1/life.asp.
For more on Louis Pasteur, see www.answersingenesis.org/creation/v14/i1/pasteur.asp.

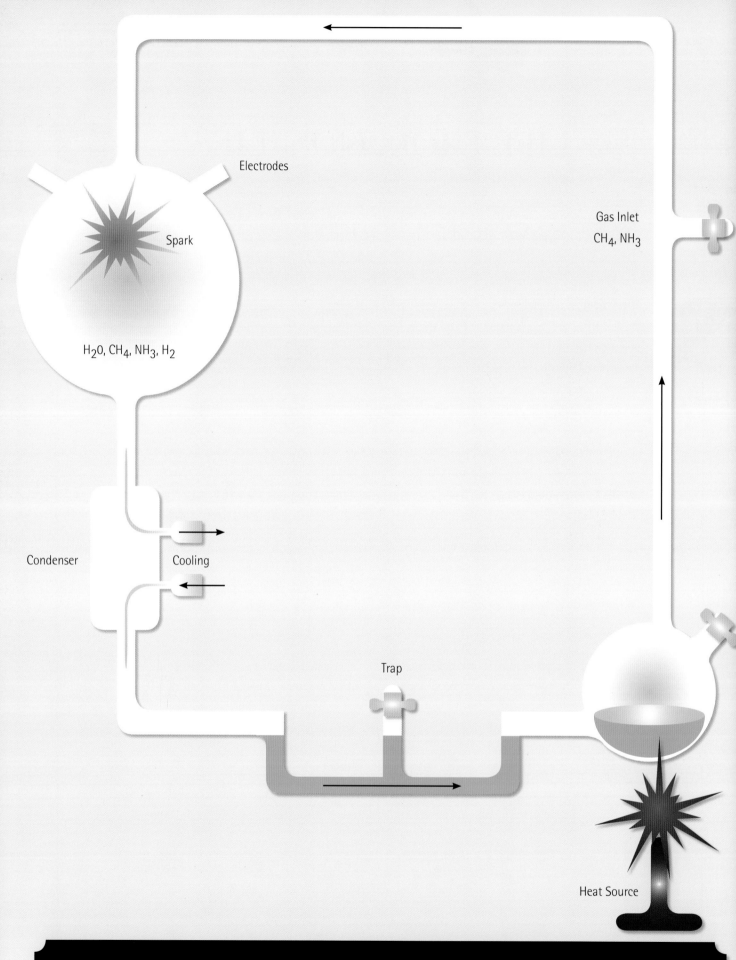

Electrodes

Spark

Gas Inlet
CH_4, NH_3

H_2O, CH_4, NH_3, H_2

Condenser

Cooling

Trap

Heat Source

The Miller-Urey experiment actually showed that abiogenesis cannot occur.

MILLER-UREY EXPERIMENT

Some museums may discuss the Miller-Urey experiment of 1953 as evidence that abiogenesis can occur. Anti-evolutionist Philip Johnson informs us:

> Because post-Darwinian biology has been dominated by materialist dogma, the biologists have had to pretend that organisms are a lot simpler than they are. Life itself must be merely chemistry. Assemble the right chemicals, and life emerges. DNA must likewise be a product of chemistry alone. As an exhibit in the New Mexico Museum of Natural History puts it, "volcanic gases plus lightning equal DNA equals LIFE!" When queried about this fable, the museum spokesman acknowledged that it was simplified but said it was basically true. (Phillip Johnson, *Weekly Wedge Update*, April 30, 2001, p. 1.)

This experiment actually showed that abiogenesis *cannot* occur.

- The Miller-Urey experiment used a methane-ammonia atmosphere, without oxygen because researchers once thought that earth's original atmosphere lacked oxygen, and oxygen was known to have detrimental effects on the experiments they were conducting. However, scientists have now found that "the accepted picture of the earth's early atmosphere has changed: It was probably O_2-rich with some nitrogen, a less reactive mixture than Miller's, or it might have been composed largely of carbon dioxide, which would greatly deter the development of organic compounds." (C. Flowers, *A Science Odyssey: 100 Years of Discovery*. New York: William Morrow and Company, 1998, p. 173.)

- In addition to producing amino acids, the experiment also produced an abundance of toxic chemicals (cyanides, carbon monoxide, etc.) that are harmful to the amino acids.

- The very forms of energy suggested to have initiated abiogenesis actually destroy the amino acids formed in the process. The experimenters built a trap in the apparatus to collect the formed amino acids to prevent that destruction. No such trap existed in the supposed primordial earth.

- Naturalistic philosopher Karl Popper remarks: "What makes the origin of life and of the genetic code a disturbing riddle is this: the genetic code is without any biological function unless it is translated; that is, unless it leads to the synthesis of the proteins whose structure is laid down by the code. But ... the machinery by which the cell (at least the non-primitive cell, which is the only one we know) translates the code consists of at least fifty macromolecular components which are themselves coded in the DNA. Thus the code can not be translated except by using certain products of its translation. This constitutes a baffling circle; a really vicious circle, it seems, for any attempt to form a model or theory of the genesis of the genetic code." (Karl Popper, "Scientific reduction and the essential incompleteness of all science" in Francisco Ayala and Theodosius Dobzhansky, eds., *Studies in the Philosophy of Biology*. Berkeley: University of California Press, 1974, p. 270.)

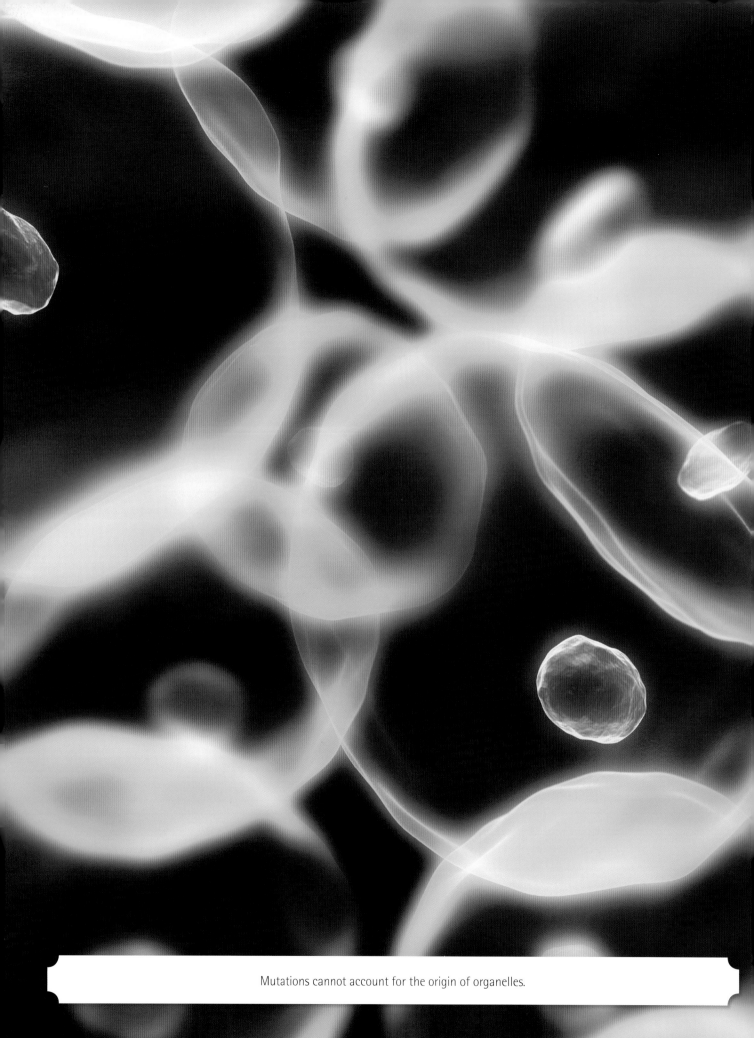

Mutations cannot account for the origin of organelles.

ENDOSYMBIOSIS?

Did the first cells begin when they gobbled up other cells?

Molecular geneticist Dr. Georgia Purdom says,

> Organelles such as mitochondria and plastids have extremely integrated and complex relationships with other parts of the cell where they reside. One of those relationships is the ability to transport organelle proteins that are encoded by genes in the nucleus and formed in other parts of the cell back into the organelle where they are needed for the organelle's proper functioning.
>
> The transport pathway is composed of many proteins that work together to bring the protein into the organelle. Each organelle has specific pathways (which differ between organelles) to accomplish this, and there are typically several different pathways needed to bring a variety of proteins into the organelle. For example, five pathways have been identified so far for transport of proteins into mitochondria. Each pathway is composed of several proteins; some are shared among the pathways, while others are unique to a pathway. The case is similar for plastids.
>
> Mutations cannot account for the origin of these protein-transport pathways. If there is no way to form these pathways, then the organelles would become obsolete once they started transferring their genes to the nucleus. Furthermore, if there was no pathway to return the proteins to the organelle, then the organelles would stop functioning and would no longer be selected for because they did not serve a purpose.

For more information, see www.answersingenesis.org/cec/docs/endosymbiotic-theory.asp.

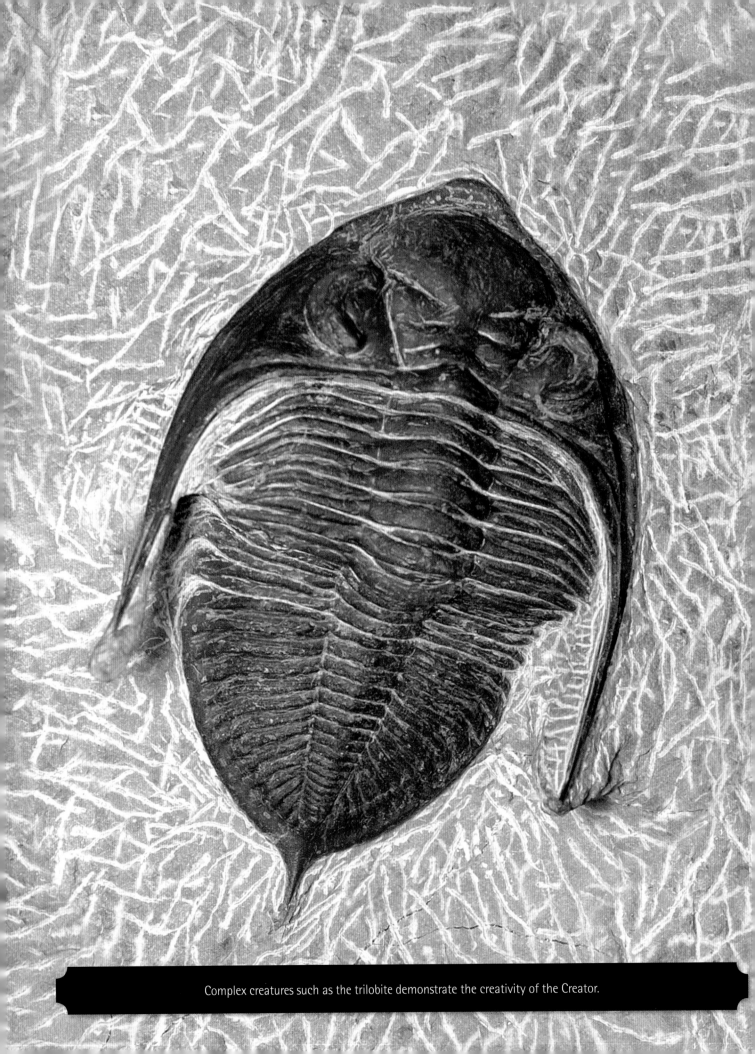

Complex creatures such as the trilobite demonstrate the creativity of the Creator.

THE CAMBRIAN EXPLOSION

Did life suddenly explode on the scene during the Cambrian Period?

Actually, rather than representing a snapshot of life 500–600 million years ago, this layer of rock represents a snapshot of a series of marine ecosystems that were buried in the beginning stages of the Flood 4,300 years ago.

Paleontologist Dr. Kurt Wise suggests that as you look at the museum mural of the "Cambrian Explosion," you should think of it as a picture of life before the Flood. He points out that the animals found in this layer are complex, completely formed, and are part of fully integrated ecosystems of marvelous beauty and wonder, reflective of the nature of the Creator. Some of the animals buried in Cambrian rocks are part of huge groups of thousands of species completely unknown in the present, like the trilobites, the sponge-like archaeocyathans, the crusting-algae-like stromatoporoids, and the tabulate and rugosan corals. Others (echinoderms, the mollusks, and the brachiopods) are broadly classified in modern groups but showed a much greater diversity than we observe in the present. Other animals, especially those buried in Ediacaran rocks just below the Cambrian, are just plain weird, like the Ediacaran and Tommotian faunas.

From the beginning, God created animals with the ability to reproduce other like themselves.

REPRODUCTIVE HABBITS

How did sexual reproduction come about?

Richard Dawkins, a leading evolutionary proponent, says:

> To say, as I have, that good genes can benefit from the existence of sex whereas bad genes can benefit from its absence, is not the same thing as explaining why sex is there at all. There are many theories of why sex exists, and none of them is knock-down convincing. (Richard Dawkins, *Climbing Mount Improbable*. Harmondsworth, UK: Penguin Books, 1997, p. 75.)

Consider the scenario required for sexual reproduction to develop. Two individuals of the same species need to acquire the mutations that lead to each only passing on half of their chromosomes (in a very complex process known as meiosis) at the same time and place in history. They need to develop male and female sex organs, and everything associated with these complex reproductive organs. These two individuals then need to find each other and mate. The two cells need to be able to combine together to form a new life.

While the advantages to sexual reproduction are often provided as evidence for evolution, the mechanism is rarely explained. A seeming advantage does not require that it develop in the first place. Additionally, sexual reproduction is more costly and less efficient than asexual reproduction—so how can sexual reproduction be an advantage?

The ability to reproduce sexually or asexually is difficult to explain within a non-biblical worldview. Of course, we know from the Bible that God created things to produce "after their kind" (see Genesis 1).

Then God said: "Let the waters abound with an abundance of living creatures ..." Gen. 1:20a

OCEAN LIFE EXHIBITS

"Nobody understands the origin of life. If they say they do, they are probably trying to fool you."

DID WE COME FROM THE OCEAN?

According to evolutionary natural history, at some point the molten earth cooled and oceans formed. As rain fell, chemicals in a hypothetical pool, warmed by the volcanic activity and energized by lightning, organized into proteins, lipids, and carbohydrates. These molecules then organized into cellular structures like proteins, DNA, and cell membranes, which then became the first living creature.

The problem with this evolutionary scenario is that chemistry prohibits it. Proteins do not form from piles of amino acids, and they cannot form in water because the water breaks the bonds that hold the amino acids together.

The DNA that tells the amino acids how to come together to form proteins contains a specific code that must be copied from another strand of DNA. Where did the information for the original DNA strand come from? Scientists have shown that information can't originate by itself from matter.

Recently, a hypothesis involving bubbles from deep ocean vents was suggested to explain how life originated. However, the same chemistry limitations mentioned in the previous paragraph apply.

Ken Nealson, a geobiologist of the University of Southern California and a NASA astrobiologist at the Jet Propulsion Laboratory in Pasadena, CA, stated:

> Nobody understands the origin of life. If they say they do, they are probably trying to fool you. (www.space.com/scienceastronomy/astronomy/odds_of_et_020521-1.html)

Of course, from a biblical perspective, we know that God created living animals and plants according to their "kinds" in the beginning (Genesis 1).

The alleged similarities between our blood and seawater simply aren't there!

IS OUR BLOOD SIMILAR TO SEA WATER?

The claim that the composition of blood is similar to sea water is based on the assumption that life came from the ocean. The following table shows that, contrary to what some may claim, the similarities between our blood and seawater are simply not there. However, even if blood and sea water were similar, this wouldn't prove one came from the other.

The information in the chart was taken from:

- C.A. Burtis and E.R. Ashwood, *Clinical Chemistry*. Philadelphia: W.B. Saunders Company, 1994 edition.
- R.C. Baselt and R.H. Cravey, *Disposition of toxic drugs and chemicals in Man*. Chicago: Year Book Medical Publ., 1989 edition.
- *The New Encyclopædia Britannica*, **15**:925, 1992, 15th ed.

Element	Blood	Seawater
Sodium	3220 mg/liter	10800
Chlorine	3650	19400
Potassium	200	392
Calcium	50	411
Magnesium	27	1290
Phosphorus	36	0.09
Iron	1	0.004
Copper	1	0.001
Zinc	1.1	0.005
Chromium	1.1	0.0002
Bromine	4	67
Fluorine	0.1	1.3
Boron	1	5
Selenium	0.9	0.0001

Even the largest coral reefs could have formed in the 4,300 years since the Flood.

HOW LONG DOES IT TAKE FOR A CORAL REEF TO GROW?

If the earth is no more than 6,000 years old, and the Flood disrupted ocean life 4,300 years ago, can coral reef "ages" of tens of thousands of years be correct?

The suggested rates of .003–3.1 inches/year (.08–80 mm/year) are far less than actual recorded rates of growth based on soundings, which reveal annual growth rates of 11–16 inches (280–414 mm). With the right amount of light and water temperature, coral can grow much faster than some have suggested. With these growth rates, even the largest coral reefs could have formed in the 4,300 years since the Flood.

For more information, see www.grisda.org/origins/06088.htm.

Whales have many unique features not found in land mammals,
making it difficult to believe they evolved from a land animal.

WHALE "EVOLUTION"?

Whales are thought by evolutionists to have evolved from land mammals. Many museums present a nice, orderly succession of fossils that supposedly show this transition from land to water. However there are many problems with the idea that a land animal could turn into a water mammal.

- Whales do not have the pelvis that land mammals do. If they did, they would crush it with the movements of their tails. How does the pelvis of a land mammal slowly shrink while at the same time maintaining itself as a viable animal?
- The nostrils would have had to migrate from the front of the face to the top of the skull.
- Significant changes in the internal breathing system to allow the animals to hold their breath for long periods and for the baby whales to drink milk while swimming under water would need to be made.
- The skin would need to lose hair and sweat glands and incorporate fibrous, fatty blubber.
- Whales have a water echo-location system lacking in land mammals.
- Whales have unique hearing systems, with no opening to the exterior.

For more information, see www.answersingenesis.org/go/whales.

Remember, God created the sea creatures (including the whale kind) on Day 5. He created the land creatures on Day 6.

The alleged vestigial hind legs found buried in the flesh of whales are different in males and females. They help to strengthen the whale's reproductive organs.

WHAT ARE THEY, REALLY?

- The alleged vestigial hind legs found buried in the flesh of whales are different in males and females and help strengthen the whale's reproductive organs.

- *Ambulocetus*

  The fossilized bones that were found suggest that this was a land-dwelling creature, not an intermediate transitional form. Concerning this fossil, the evolutionary biologist Annalisa Berta commented:

  > Since the pelvic girdle is not preserved, there is no direct evidence in *Ambulocetus* for a connection between the hind limbs and the axial skeleton. This hinders interpretations of locomotion in this animal, since many of the muscles that support and move the hindlimb originate on the pelvis. (J.G.M. Thewissen, S.T. Hussain, and M. Arif, "Fossil Evidence for the Origin of Aquatic Locomotion in Archeocete Whales," *Science* **263**:5144, January 14, 1994, pp. 210-212. A Berta, "Perspective: What is a Whale?," same issue, pp. 180-181.)

  Even with the 1996 discovery of parts of the pelvis, the evidence still indicates that this creature was a land-dwelling animal.

- *Basilosaurus*

  This fossil had functional hind limbs, which were probably used for grasping in reproduction. It was a fully aquatic sea mammal. Evolutionary vertebrate paleontologist Barbara Stahl stated:

  > "The serpentine form of the body and the peculiar shape of the cheek teeth make it plain that these archaeocetes [like *Basilosaurus*] could not possibly have been the ancestor of modern whales." (B.J. Stahl, *Vertebrate History: Problems in Evolution*. New York: McGraw-Hill, 1974, p. 489.)

- *Pakicetus*

  The original fossil find consisted only of jaw and skull fragments. Its hearing system was the same as other land mammals, and it was found in the same sediments as other land-dwelling creatures. In later discoveries, it was found that:

  > "All the postcranial bones indicate that pakicetids were land mammals, and ... indicate that the animals were runners, with only their feet touching the ground." (C. de Muizon, "Walking with whales," *Nature* **413**, September 29, 2001, pp. 259-260.)

This dinosaur model, featured in the Creation Museum (www.creationmuseum.org),
will point people to the true history of the world found in the Bible.

DINOSAUR EXHIBITS

Dragon legends and sculptures are found around the world.

DINOSAURS AND DRAGONS

In 1841, Sir Richard Owen coined the term "dinosaur" (meaning "terrible lizard") for the great beasts that were being rediscovered at that time. Yes, that's right, *re*discovered. You see, Adam and Eve were the first people to discover dinosaurs as they walked with them in the Garden of Eden, 6,000 years ago. In the beginning, man and all animals—including all the dinosaur kinds—were on a strict vegetarian diet (Genesis 1:29–30). That changed sometime after the Fall, which is why some dinosaurs are now classified as meat-eaters.

Two of each kind of dinosaur survived the global Flood by riding safely on the Ark. After the Flood, people continued to live in close proximity to dinosaurs. Many tales of their adventures have been passed down in the form of legends about dragons. In fact, most of the older translations of the Bible (e.g., the King James Version) mention dragons in several places.

- Thou didst divide the sea by thy strength: thou brakest the heads of the dragons in the waters. (Psalm 74:13)

- And I hated Esau, and laid his mountains and his heritage waste for the dragons of the wilderness. (Malachi 1:3)

- In that day the LORD with his sore and great and strong sword shall punish leviathan the piercing serpent, even leviathan that crooked serpent; and he shall slay the dragon that is in the sea. (Isaiah 27:1)

- And the wild asses did stand in the high places, they snuffed up the wind like dragons; their eyes did fail, because there was no grass. (Jeremiah 14:6)

- The beast of the field shall honour me, the dragons and the owls: because I give waters in the wilderness, and rivers in the desert, to give drink to my people, my chosen. (Isaiah 43:20)

Other people drew pictures of their encounters with the feared beasts on rock surfaces and cave walls. Still others carved their likeness into stone (for example, on the leaning tower of Pisa), painted them into pictures, and engraved them in brass (such as at the tomb of Bishop Bell in England).

For more information, visit www.answersingenesis.org/go/dragons.

Are dinosaurs really extinct, or do they still roam remote parts of the earth?

WHERE ARE THE GREAT BEASTS TODAY?

Several animals that were once thought to be extinct are now known to be alive (for example, the coelacanth). In recent years there has been intriguing testimony from people living near the dense jungles of central Africa and New Guinea to suggest that dinosaurs might still be alive. But we need more evidence to be sure.

If dinosaurs are indeed extinct, did they die out when a giant meteor slammed into the earth about 65 million years ago? Did they evolve into birds? (See p. 63 for the answer.) These are the stories evolutionists tell us in the secular natural history museums. The truth is that, if they are truly extinct, the evidence presented previously (e.g., dragon legends, possible eye-witness reports) indicates that they died out sometime over the past few hundred or thousand years since the Flood. And this would have likely been caused by the same factors that cause many animals to go extinct today: loss of habitat and food supply, disease, climate change, hunting pressures by man or other animals, etc.

There are many problems with the impact theory for dinosaur extinction. As you learn about this idea from the museum, consider the following points that have been made by evolutionists Charles Officer and Jake Page in *The Great Dinosaur Extinction Controversy*. Addison-Wesley, 1996:

- The number of dinosaurs declines gradually as one goes upward through the fossil record, rather than all at once, as the impact theory would suggest.
- Many species of animals that require light survived the alleged impact and the subsequent darkening of the skies that supposedly resulted from the impact debris.

For more information, see www.answersingenesis.org/go/dinosaurs.

Apatosaurs, diplodocoids, tyrannosaurs, and dromaeosaurs have hips structured similarly to lizards.

LIZARD OR BIRD HIPS?

Before 1888, paleontologists classified the many different dinosaurs in various ways: sometimes according to tooth structure, sometimes according to foot structure. In 1888, British paleontologist Harry Seeley gave a lecture in which he proposed that dinosaurs should be grouped according to the structure of their pelvic bones and joints. The saurischian dinosaurs are "lizard-hipped," while the ornithischian dinosaurs are "bird-hipped."

The dinosaurs with hips structured similarly to lizards include the great sauropods (e.g., apatosaurs, brachiosaurs, and diplodocoids), and the carnivorous theropods (e.g., tyrannosaurs, and dromaeosaurs). The dinosaurs with hips that are more similar to birds in design include the stegosaurs, ceratops, hadrosaurs, and pachycephalosaurs.

Although one may be inclined to think (within an evolutionary worldview) that birds have evolved from bird-hipped dinosaurs, this is in fact not the case. Evolutionary scientists suggest that *theropods* are the main ancestors of today's birds.

However, as will be seen on the following pages, the idea that dinosaurs and birds share a common ancestor is not scientifically viable.

We know from the Bible that birds were created a day before dinosaurs, and thus birds cannot be descended from them.

DID DINOSAURS HAVE FEATHERS?

In many museums, the curators have fashioned some dinosaurs with feather-like coverings, instead of scales. This is mainly due to their belief that dinosaurs are the ancestors of birds. However, we know from the Bible that birds were created a day *before* dinosaurs, and therefore cannot be their descendants.

Although it may be possible that God created some reptiles with feathers, this would showcase the creativity of the Creator. It is not evidence for the genetic information increase that would be needed for reptiles to turn into birds.

A November 1999 *National Geographic* article ("Feathers for T. rex?" **196**:5, pp. 98–107) illustrated a baby *T. rex* and a *Deinonychus* with feathers. In a prominent heading, the article proclaimed: "We can now say that birds are theropods just as confidently as we say that humans are mammals." This was based on a fossil illegally exported from Liaoning Province, China, tentatively named *Archaeoraptor liaoningensis*, allegedly a "feathered dinosaur." It was later found that Archaeoraptor was a fraud—a combination of a bird-like creature's head and a dinosaur tail. In a letter to *National Geographic* over the *Archaeoraptor* scandal, Dr. Storrs Olson (curator of birds at the Smithsonian) wrote:

> The idea of feathered dinosaurs and the theropod origin of birds is being actively promulgated by a cadre of zealous scientists acting in concert with certain editors at Nature and National Geographic who themselves have become outspoken and highly biased proselytizers of the faith. Truth and careful scientific weighing of evidence have been among the first casualties in their program, which is now fast becoming one of the grander scientific hoaxes of our age—the paleontological equivalent of cold fusion.

His entire letter is reprinted at www.answersingenesis.org/docs/4159.asp.

Birds are dinosaurs? Hardly!

DID DINOSAURS TURN INTO BIRDS?

In addition to the biblical teaching, there are many scientific problems with the dino-bird idea.

- The lungs of reptiles and birds are structured differently. Dinosaurs (reptiles) have bellows-like lungs (the air is pumped in and out), as humans do. Birds have a circulatory lung, in which the air flows through the lung, without being pumped. Evolutionist Dr. Michael Denton has said, "It doesn't require a great deal of profound knowledge of biology to see that for an organ which is so central to the physiology of any higher organism, its drastic modification in that way by a series of small events is almost inconceivable. This is something we can't throw under the carpet again because, basically, as Darwin said, if any organ can be shown to be incapable of being achieved gradually in little steps, his theory would be totally overthrown." (See www.answersingenesis.org/creation/v21/i4/design.asp.)

- According to evolutionist Dr. Alan Feduccia, "New research shows that birds lack the embryonic thumb that dinosaurs had, suggesting that it is 'almost impossible' for the species to be closely related." *(The Cincinnati Enquirer*, October 25, 1997)

- Birds have streamlined bodies, enabling them to be efficient flyers. In addition, most have hollow bones, which make them lightweight, and which are part of their respiratory system. They also have powerful flight muscles. Reptiles lack these features.

- Although some museums may claim that feathers are merely modified scales, careful research has shown this is not true.

Anatomist Dr. David Menton describes the most fundamental difference between feathers and scales: "The feather grows out of a follicle. A follicle is a tubular down-growth of the epidermis that protrudes deeply into the skin—all the way down to underlying bone in the case of primary feathers. And this tube of specialized living skin produces the feather inside of itself from a growth matrix at the very bottom. The reptilian scale has absolutely nothing to do with follicles. All of the scales can shed as a sheet because they're nothing but folds in the epidermis, like fabric folded over on itself, whereas feathers would have to come out of their own follicle." ("Bird evolution flies out the window," *Creation* **6**(4), September 1994, pp. 16–19.) Add to that the findings by evolutionists: "At the morphological level feathers are traditionally considered homologous with reptilian scales. However, in development, morphogenesis, gene structure, protein shape and sequence, and filament formation and structure, feathers are different." (A.H. Brush, "On the origin of feathers," *Journal of Evolutionary Biology* **9**, 1996, pp. 131–142.)

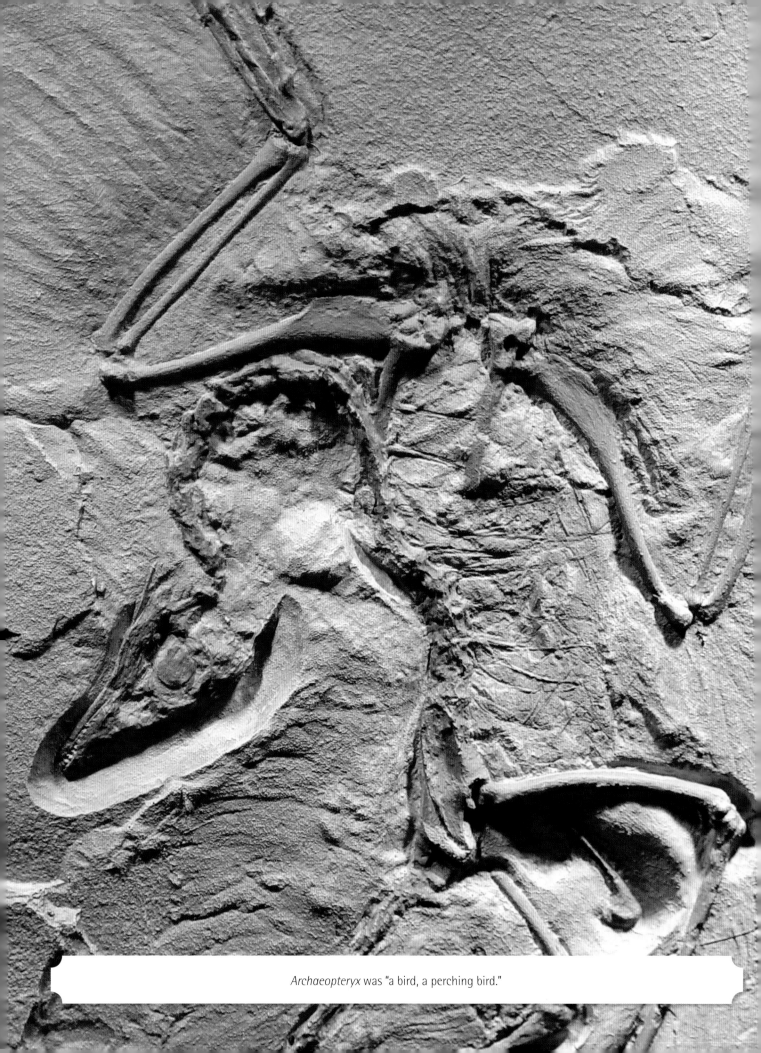

Archaeopteryx was "a bird, a perching bird."

WHAT ARE THEY, REALLY?

In evaluating the alleged transitional forms, it can sometimes be difficult to separate fact from fiction. Did the fossil have feathers or were the "feathers" simply frayed collagen fibers? Was it an actual bird or some type of reptile?

Without access to the original specimens themselves, we can only base our conclusions on highly interpretive articles *about* the fossils. If your museum displays casts of the original fossils, spend most of your time looking at these, rather than at the showcases of someone's imagination.

Archaeopteryx

World-renowned evolutionary ornithologist, Dr. Alan Feduccia, has said, "Paleontologists have tried to turn *Archaeopteryx* into an earth-bound, feathered dinosaur. But it's not. It is a bird, a perching bird. And no amount of 'paleobabble' is going to change that." (Alan Feduccia, quoted in V. Morell, "Archaeopteryx: Early Bird Catches a Can of Worms," *Science* **259**:5096, February 5, 1993, pp. 764–765.)

For example, *Archaeopteryx* had:

- the special avian lung design that modern birds have.
- the same brain as modern birds have, with a large cerebellum and visual cortex.
- lower and upper jaws that moved, as modern birds do (only the lower jaw moves in reptiles).
- grasping teeth as other fossil birds did.
- a robust wishbone (furcula), as modern birds do.
- a grasping hallux (hind toe), as do modern perching birds.

Bambiraptor feinbergi

Although frequently illustrated with feathers, none were actually found on the 95-percent-complete *Bambiraptor* skeleton! Wes Linster, a fourteen year-old fossil hunter, discovered the unusually complete *Bambiraptor* skeleton in 1995, while he was searching in Glacier National Park (Montana, USA). Although *Bambiraptor*, a small theropod dinosaur, is claimed to be an *ancestor* of birds, it has been given an age of 75 million years *younger* than the true bird *Archaeopteryx*.

Caudipteryx zoui

Evolutionary ornithologists Larry Martin and Alan Feduccia believe that this specimen is more likely to be a flightless bird similar to an ostrich. *Caudipteryx* even used gizzard stones like modern plant-eating birds, but unlike theropods (www.answersingenesis.org/docs/3378.asp).

Confuciusornis

The *Confuciusornis* genus is a group of birds, the fossils of which have been found mainly in China. Some in this variety had long tail feathers, and large claws on their forelimbs. Some scientists believe these birds may have been flightless (en.wikipedia.org/wiki/Confuciusornis). Interestingly, some modern birds possess wing claws at certain stages in their life cycles: the ostrich, emu, hoatzin, moorhen, and coot.

Microraptor gui

Anatomist Dr. David Menton wrote, "There is no question that *M. gui* had true pennaceous feathers essentially identical to those of modern birds. ... The microraptors themselves, including *M. gui*, are more like birds than theropod dinosaurs. If we compare the hands of *Microraptor* to *Archaeopteryx*, for example, we find the same bird-like phalangeal formula for their digits (2-3-4)" (www.answersingenesis. org/articles/am/v2/n1/microraptor-gui). Dr. Alan Feduccia *et al.* have concluded that "the microraptors of China are birds, regardless of their ancestry" (A. Feduccia, T. Lingham-Soliar, & J.R. Hinchliffe, J *Morphol* **266**, 2005, p. 162).

Mononykus

This creature was a small theropod dinosaur that had one large claw in its forelimbs. It also had a keeled sternum, as birds do, leading some to postulate a link between the two. However, keeled sternums are also found in moles, and enable them to be strong diggers.

Protarchaeopteryx robusta

This creature had true feathers, and according to some evolutionists, was most likely a flightless bird, similar to the ostrich. It had birdlike teeth and lacked the long tail seen in theropods (J. Bergman, "The evolution of feathers: a major problem for Darwinism," TJ 17:1, April 2003, pp. 33–41, online at www. answersingenesis.org/tj/v17/i1/feathers.asp).

Protopteryx fengningensis

According to the scientists who reported this fossil, *Protopteryx* was a true flying bird. Its fossil showed imprints of downy feathers, and it had a procoracoid process on its pelvis, which indicates flight ability in modern birds (Fucheng Zhang and Zhonghe Zhou, "A primitive enantiornithine bird and the origin of feathers," *Science* **290**:5498, December 8, 2000, pp. 1955–1959).

Sinosauropteryx prima

Enough of this creature's lung structure was preserved to show that it had the bellows-like lung of reptiles, rather than the flow-through lung structure of birds. Additionally, according to four leading paleontologists (including John Ostrom from Yale), the "feathers" found with this dinosaur were actually a parallel array of fibers, probably collagen, rather than true feathers (*New Scientist* **154**:2077, April 12, 1997, p. 13).

Unenlagia comahuensis

This dinosaur had a unique shoulder joint that was highly mobile and seemingly quite bird-like. However, its body was too large to lift off the ground in flight. Since we are not able to observe how this creature moved, we cannot know for sure how it used its shoulder.

Regarding this fossil's place in the dino-to-bird transition, evolutionist Peter Dodson stated:

> I hasten to add that none of the known small theropods, including D*einonychus, Dromaeosaurus, Velociraptor, Unenlagia,* nor *Sinosauropteryx, Protarcheaeopteryx,* nor *Caudipteryx* is itself relevant to the origin of birds; these are all Cretaceous fossils ... and as such can at best represent only structural stages through which an avian ancestor may be hypothesized to have passed. (P. Dodson, "Origin of birds: the final solution?" *American Zoologist* **40**, 2000, pp. 505–506.)

For more information, see www.answersingenesis.org/tj/v17/i1/bird.asp.

Dinosaur fossils provide a snapshot of the death of that particular dinosaur, not a comprehensive picture of the dinosaur's life!

AGE OF THE DINOSAURS?

Throughout your journey in the dinosaur halls, you'll read a lot about the "age of the dinosaurs," with terms like Triassic, Jurassic, and Cretaceous periods, and phrases like "millions of years ago."

Keep in mind that much of what you're reading is evolution-based storytelling, and not actual fact. Remember, scientists do not find dinosaur bones with attached tags that say, "Hi, I'm 178 million years old." These ages are *interpretations*.

The fossils that have been found provide a snapshot of the *death* of that particular dinosaur—not a comprehensive picture of the dinosaur's *life*. Most creationists believe that the various layers in which different dinosaurs are found represent different stages of burial during the Flood (4,300 years ago).

Additionally, contrary to what the museums may be telling you, fossilization does not require long time periods—simply the right conditions. In fact, fossilization usually requires very little time. Otherwise the evidence of skin, bones, eggs, footprints, etc. would be erased by scavengers, micro-organisms, weathering, and other decay processes.

In fact, scientists have recently discovered that some *Tyrannosaurus rex* bones may still have soft tissue in them. This confirms that the bones can't be millions of years old, because the soft tissue would have decayed long ago. For more information, see www.answersingenesis.org/docs2005/0328discovery.asp.

"Look now at the behemoth ..."

DINOSAURS AND THE BIBLE

As you stand in front of an *Apatosaurus*, or similar type of dinosaur, read these words that God spoke to Job (Job 40:6–24, NKJV):

Then the Lord answered Job out of the whirlwind, and said:

"Now prepare yourself like a man; I will question you, and you shall answer Me:

"Would you indeed annul My judgment? Would you condemn Me that you may be justified?

Have you an arm like God? Or can you thunder with a voice like His?

Then adorn yourself with majesty and splendor, And array yourself with glory and beauty.

Disperse the rage of your wrath; Look on everyone who is proud, and humble him.

Look on everyone who is proud, and bring him low; Tread down the wicked in their place.

Hide them in the dust together, Bind their faces in hidden darkness.

Then I will also confess to you That your own right hand can save you.

"Look now at the behemoth, which I made along with you; He eats grass like an ox.

See now, his strength is in his hips, And his power is in his stomach muscles.

He moves his tail like a cedar; The sinews of his thighs are tightly knit.

His bones are like beams of bronze, His ribs like bars of iron.

He is the first of the ways of God; Only He who made him can bring near His sword.

Surely the mountains yield food for him, And all the beasts of the field play there.

He lies under the lotus trees, In a covert of reeds and marsh.

The lotus trees cover him with their shade; The willows by the brook surround him.

Indeed the river may rage, Yet he is not disturbed;

He is confident, though the Jordan gushes into his mouth, Though he takes it in his eyes,

Or one pierces his nose with a snare."

Some study Bible notes state that behemoth could be an elephant or a hippo. Compare the tail in front of you with the description given in Job and remember what the scrawny tail on a hippo or elephant looks like.

All mammals, like this panda, have a four-chambered heart.

MAMMAL EXHIBITS

The ancestors of mammals that fly in the air, like this bat, were created on Day 5.

MAMMALS

From the tiny, gray mouse to the large, blue whale, mammals are found on every continent and in every ocean on earth. Scientists have discovered that this group of animals shares several common characteristics: a backbone, hair (or fur) covering the body, production of milk by the female to nourish her young, and three tiny bones in the middle ear. All mammals also have a four-chambered heart, a neocortex (the special area of the brain, which is involved in higher functions such as conscious thought, spatial reasoning, sensory perception, and language [in humans]), and specialized teeth.

Although the museums will tell you that the characteristics common to all mammals are a result of sharing a common ancestor, this is not true. This "design economy" points to a single common designer.

The 152 families within the mammalian class probably represent 150–160 original "kinds" of mammals. The ancestors of those mammal kinds that live in the sea (e.g., whales) and fly in the air (e.g., bats) were created on Day 5, while those that live on the land were created on Day 6.

Scientists have grouped mammals into three main categories: monotremes (e.g., platypuses, echidnas), marsupials (e.g., opossums, kangaroos, wombats), and placentals (e.g., humans, mice, horses).

Echidnas are mammals that lay eggs rather than give birth to live young.

MONOTREMES

As mammals, the echidna and platypus share the characteristics common to other mammals: backbone, hair, milk glands, large brain. As monotremes, these unique animals are the only mammals that lay eggs, rather than giving birth to live young.

Did they evolve there?

Today, Australia is the only continent where monotremes live although fossil platypus teeth have been found in South America. Because monotremes are limited to Australia, some have claimed that this indicates they evolved there.

However, we know from the Bible that representatives of all land animals (including monotremes and marsupials) were on the Ark, which landed in the Middle East. Although monotremes may have migrated to various parts of the world after coming off the Ark (along with all the other kinds of land animals and birds), it seems they have only survived in Australia. When sea levels rose as the ice began to melt at the end of the Ice Age, Australia was cut off from the rest of the world, effectively trapping the animals that were already there.

Since the interior of Australia was much more lush during the Ice Age that followed the Flood, the ancestral platypuses would not have needed to cross today's desert in order to reach their current place of residency in Tasmania, and along the eastern seaboard of Australia. Additionally, fossil evidence indicates that the platypus was much more robust in the past—it was larger, and adults had teeth (today, the young platypuses shed their teeth before they become adults). Another thing to note is that even the "oldest" (by evolutionary dating methods) fossils of platypuses are still that—fossils of platypuses. They do not show evidence of transitioning to or from another kind of animal.

Most of the world's marsupials, like these kangaroos, are today found only in Australia.

MARSUPIALS

Marsupials differ from other mammals in that the female gives birth to live young at a very early stage in its development. Using its God-given instincts, the young makes its way into a pouch on the mother's abdomen, where it develops further before it is ready for independent living. Some marsupials have forward-facing pouches (kangaroos), while others have rear-facing pouches (wombats).

Is specialization evidence of evolution?

Some marsupials have very specialized diets. For example, the koala feasts mainly on leaves from eucalyptus trees. They have a unique way of metabolizing a plant that can be toxic in large quantities to many other animals (although, interestingly, koalas fed by hand from bottles have been known to survive on non-eucalypt diets).

We've already learned that all land animals (including the koala and panda ancestors) came off the Ark, which had landed in the mountains somewhere in the Middle East around 4,300 years ago. From there, the animals spread to various parts of the earth. Today, the koala thrives in the eucalyptus forests of Australia, while the panda lives in the mountainous regions of China.

It may be that, in the past, koalas (and other "specialized" animals of today) were more robust and were able to feast on a greater variety of foods. Over time, these animals have lost the ability to digest many foods, and now subsist only on their current diet. This is not an example of onward-upward evolution, however. Instead, it reflects a downhill change in animal populations.

Female humans bear live young which are nourished in the womb by a placenta.

PLACENTALS

Placentals are mammals that bear live young, which are nourished in the womb by a placenta. According to Dr. David Menton (a cell biologist and emeritus professor of human anatomy at Washington University Medical School in St. Louis), this amazing organ functions as the developing baby's kidneys, lungs, digestive system, liver, and immune system. The placenta also protects "the developing baby from an attack by the mother's immune system, since the baby and the placenta are genetically unique and distinctly different from the mother." (David Menton, "The Placenta: a selfless servant," *Answers Magazine* **2**:1, 2007, p. 72.)

Offspring of placentals are born more fully developed than those of the marsupial mammals.

The original members of the horse kind were created by God on Day 6, 6,000 years ago.

HORSE "EVOLUTION"?

One of the more famous so-called "evidences" for molecules-to-man evolution is the horse series. Some creationist believe that, following the Flood, today's horses may have rapidly diversified within the horse kind that was represented on the Ark. However, this diversification within a "kind" does not provide evidence for particles-to-people evolution. Instead, it follows from the Bible-based teaching that animals reproduce according to their kind.

Drs. Cavanaugh, Wood, and Wise analyzed 19 fossil horse species. Their statistical analysis revealed that significant similarity exists among the fossils. They concluded that all nineteen species (including *Hyracotherium, Epihippus, Orohippus, Anchitherium, Megahippus, Hypohippus, Merychipuus, Pliohippus,* and *Protohippus*) belong to the same "horse kind." They interpret this as a record of post-Flood diversification within the kind. (D. Cavanaugh, T. Wood (Ph.D., biochemistry), K. Wise (Ph.D., paleontology), "Fossil Equidae: A Monobaraminic, Stratomorphic Series," *Proceedings of the Fifth International Conference on Creationism,* Creation Science Fellowship, 2003, pp. 143–153)

- Horses today range in size from the small miniature horse to the large Clydesdale. Additionally, some horses today are born with more than one toe. Horses further vary in their number of ribs, from 17–19 pairs.
- Some have suggested that horse splint bones are evolutionary leftovers. However, scientists have recently found that the splint bones play an important role in strengthening the leg and foot bones, providing an attachment point for muscles, and protecting the suspensory ligament. (J. Sarfati, "Useless horse body parts? No way!" *Creation* **24**:3, June 2000, pp. 24–25.)

Red-eyed tree frogs are found in the rainforests of Costa Rica and Central America.

REPTILE AND AMPHIBIAN EXHIBITS

Fossil and genetic evidence support the biblically-based notion that amphibians, such as these newts, have always been amphibians, and reptiles have always been reptiles

AMPHIBIAN: THE TRANSITION FROM FISH TO REPTILE?

Amphibian characteristics are claimed to be intermediate between fish and reptiles. However, there are several major hurdles that need to be overcome in order for this supposed evolutionary transformation to happen: skin needs to change, amniotic egg needs to develop, lungs need to advance and change.

Amphibian skin contains many different glands that are not present in the reptile skin, and the reptilian scales develop from folds in the skin. So not only would amphibians need to develop the genetic information for glands (not found in fish), reptiles would also need to develop the genetic information for scales. Again, a process that increases the information content of the genome has not been observed scientifically.

Amphibians absorb and release gases through their skin as part of their respiration. Their thin, permeable skin would need to develop into the thick, waterproof skin of reptiles; so another developmental pathway would have to appear. The amphibian skin would need to lose the ability to exchange gases, and a complex lung system would need to develop in order for the "emerging" reptiles to accommodate life on dry land.

Amphibians must lay their eggs in wet environments to prevent them from drying out. Reptile eggs have a leathery covering that prevents loss of water but still allows gases to be exchanged with the environment. There is no record of the molecular and developmental changes that would have had to occur to make this transition.

Fossil and genetic evidence support the biblically-based fact that amphibians have always been amphibians and reptiles have always been reptiles—both groups were created by the Creator to inhabit the earth.

Many now-fossilized amphibians may have lived in a now-extinct floating forest ecosystem before the Flood. These unique ecosystems may have been destroyed and buried during the Flood to form thick coal seams we find in the rock record today. (K. Wise, "The Pre-Flood Floating Forest," *Proceedings of the Fifth International Conference on Creationism*, Creation Science Fellowship, 2003, pp. 371–381)

Fish did not evolve into amphibians; God created them differently!

THE DEVONIAN: DID FISH BECOME AMPHIBIANS?

Evolutionists suggest that it was during the so-called "Devonian" period that fish evolved into amphibians. The museum may even have a picture of the famous fish that crawled out onto the land.

However, another interpretation better explains the creatures found in this fossilized formation. Rather than viewing the fossils in a step-by-step evolutionary fashion, think of them as a group of animals that were buried together in the Flood, 4,300 years ago.

Paleontologist Dr. Kurt Wise believes that a massive (sub-continent to continent size) pre-Flood floating forest was buried in stages during the beginning of the Flood, and that this explains the Devonian animals (the "Devonian" was a location in the floating forest, not a place in time).

"Living among the flora of the floating forest was an associated fauna. This fauna would have ranged from fish which lived in the pools in the forest floor, to amphibians which inhabited the aquatic/terrestrial interface, to insects and small animals which lived in the terrestrial environment of the understory and canopy. The permanent destruction of the floating forest biome would explain why virtually all Paleozoic 'land' animals are extinct. It would also provide a reasonable explanation for the stratigraphic position, the environment, and the morphology of the animals which appear to be fully functional morphological intermediates between fish and amphibians (e.g., *Ichthyostega*)." (K. Wise, "The Pre-Flood Floating Forest," Proceedings of the Fifth International Conference on Creationism, Creation Science Fellowship, 2003, p. 376)

In the next three quotes, creationist geologist Paul Garner elaborates.

> The Devonian tetrapods are thought to have lived a predatory lifestyle in weed-infested shallow water. They were therefore equipped with characteristics appropriate to that habitat (e.g., crocodile-like morphology with dorsally placed eyes, limbs and tails made for swimming, internal gills, lateral line systems). Some of these features are also found in fishes that shared their environment.

Were these creatures "transitional forms"?

The mosaic pattern makes it difficult to identify organisms or groups of organisms that possess the "right" combination of characters to be considered part of an evolutionary lineage. Consider the tetrapod-like lobe-fins *Panderichthys* and *Elpistostege*. Despite their appearance, these fish have some unique characters (such as the design of the vertebrae) that rule them out as tetrapod ancestors. At best, evolutionists can only claim that they are a *model* of the kind of fish that must have served as that ancestor. ... Another example is *Livoniana*, a so-called "near tetrapod" known from two lower jaw fragments. It possesses a curious mixture of fish-like and tetrapod-like characteristics, but it also has up to five rows of teeth, a feature not seen either in the fishes from which it is thought to be descended nor the tetrapods into which it is said to be evolving. That the mosaic distribution of characters can cause great confusion is exemplified by the recent discovery of *Psarolepis*, a fish from the Upper Silurian/Lower Devonian of China, which combines characters found in placoderms, chondrichthyans, ray finned fishes, and lobe-fins.

Consider also the changes needed to go from fish to amphibians.

... in fish the head, shoulder girdle, and circulatory systems constitute a single mechanical unit. The shoulder girdle is firmly connected to the vertebral column and is an anchor for the muscles involved in lateral undulation of the body, mouth opening, heart contractions, and timing of the blood circulation through the gills. However, in amphibians the head is not connected to the shoulder girdle, in order to allow effective terrestrial feeding and locomotion. Evolutionists must suppose that the head became incrementally detached from the shoulder girdle, in a step-wise fashion, with functional intermediates at every stage. However, a satisfactory account of how this might have happened has never been given.

(Paul Garner, "The Fossil Record of 'Early' Tetrapods: Evidence of a Major Evolutionary Transition?" *TJ* **17**:2, 2003, pp. 111–117, available online at www.answersingenesis.org/tj/v17/i2/tetrapod.asp.)

MAMMAL-LIKE REPTILES: TRANSITIONAL FORMS?

Some creatures appear to have features found in both mammals and reptiles. These "mammal-like reptiles" are alleged to be the transitional forms between reptiles and mammals.. As with all alleged evolutionary transitions, evolutionists themselves are unclear about what exactly involved into what. They realize that this group of animals does not show an obvious transition from reptile to mammal.

> It is not known which cynodont [a group of mammal-like reptiles] family was ancestral to mammals, or whether all the mammals originated from the same group (family) of cynodonts. In the vast literature concerning mammalian origins, it is easier to find suggestions that one or the other therapsid or cynodont family cannot be ancestral to the Mammalia, rather than to find a positive answer. (Z. Kielan-Jaworowska, "Interrelationships of Mesozoic mammals," *Historical Biology* **6**:3, 1992, p. 195.)

Additionally, there are tremendous differences between mammals and reptiles, which cannot be accounted for by information-losing mutations or natural selection.

- They have different circulatory systems, and breathe differently (mammals have a diaphragm).
- They hear differently (mammals have an organ of corti, which reptiles lack).
- They feed their young differently (female mammals produce milk, reptiles don't).
- They have different skin structures (mammals have hair and sweat glands, which reptiles lack).
- Mammals are warm-blooded; reptiles are cold-blooded.

Futher, John Woodmorappe points out that "rather than a progression to 'mammalness,' we observe an assortment of unmistakable reptilian traits and unmistakable mammalian traits." (John Woodmorappe, "Walking whales, nested hierarchies, and chimeras: do they exist?," *TJ* **16**:1, 2002, pp. 111–119, available online at www.answersingenesis.org/tj/v16/i1/chimeras.asp.) He adds elsewhere:

> ...the traits usually considered unique to mammals are distributed variously throughout the mammal-like reptiles. While this distribution is not haphazard or random, it does *not* form lineages. ... Just because some "mammalian" traits are present in mammal-like reptiles, this does not entail evolution in the slightest. It simply means that some traits now considered mammalian (by virtue of the fact that they are found only in extinct mammals) once existed in some extinct non-mammals. (J. Woodmorappe, "Mammal-like reptiles: major trait reversals and discontinuities," *TJ* **15**:1, 2001, pp. 44–52, available online at www.answersingenesis.org/tj/v15/i1/reptiles.asp.)

Even assuming it could be established that the ancestor of snakes today had legs, creationists have no problem in principle with loss of features through natural processes.

HAVE SNAKES LOST THEIR LEGS?

The *Educator's Guide* to the American Museum of Natural History's exhibit "Lizards and Snakes: Alive!" states:

> All of the almost 8,000 living squamates [lizards and snakes] can trace their lineage back to one common ancestor that lived at least 200 million years ago. Since that time, many squamate groups have gone extinct and new groups have evolved. Dozens of squamate groups have undergone limb reduction and loss. Limblessness is an excellent adaptation to life underground, where much food is found and predators are few. Losing limbs may have allowed squamates to take advantage of resources unavailable to limbed vertebrates.

Despite no one ever observing it, descent from a common ancestor is once again assumed. Did that ancestor live on land? Or was it a marine creature? Once again, evolutionists aren't sure—yet they *are* sure that squamates have evolved from non-squamates.

So what about fossils of snakes that allegedly show snakes with limbs in the past? Even assuming it could be established that the ancestor of snakes today had legs, creationists have no problem, in principle, with loss of features through natural processes.

How creatures *lost* legs is no explanation for the *origin* of legs in the first place and is not evidence for molecules-to-man evolution, which requires addition of new genetic information. Loss of legs could be achieved through degeneration of the DNA information sequences that specify leg development.

Additionally, evolutionists themselves are confused about what this might mean. Features claimed by one group as evidence for an evolutionary relationship are claimed by other evolutionists as evidence of "convergence" (similar structures that evolved separately and are not the result of having common ancestry). Further, the "rudimentary legs" on some snakes are acknowledged as having a function during reproduction, as claspers during copulation.

Are snakes with legs evidence of the serpent in Genesis? We ought to be wary of rushing to compare such finds to the Genesis serpent. The fossils most likely formed during Noah's Flood, hence the creatures they represent were in existence some 1,600 years *after* the cursing of the serpent to crawl on its belly.

A human is not just another mammal. We were created differently from the animals!

HUMAN EXHIBITS

God created humans in His image; He gave them the responsibility of caring for His creation.

AM I AN ANIMAL?

Museums often go to great pains to emphasize that humans are just another animal, like all the other mammals in the museum.

In some ways, we are like other mammals: we have a backbone, our bodies are covered with hair, we have three middle ear bones, our hearts have four chambers, and our brains are covered by a neocortex. Other animals communicate with each other, as we do (though human communication even in the infant stage is vastly more complex than any animal communication). Some animals use tools, as we do.

In other more important ways, we are not like mammals or other animals at all.

- God created humans in His image (Genesis 1:26–27).
- God specially created humans from the dust of the ground (Genesis 2:7).
- We have the capability to spend eternity with our Creator (Ecclesiastes 3:11).
- We can read and write.
- We use tools to make other tools.
- Jesus Christ came to die for the sin of *humans*—not animals.

We're not just another mammal; we were created in the image of God. We were given the assignment to rule over the rest of creation, under the authority of God and according to His instructions in Scripture.

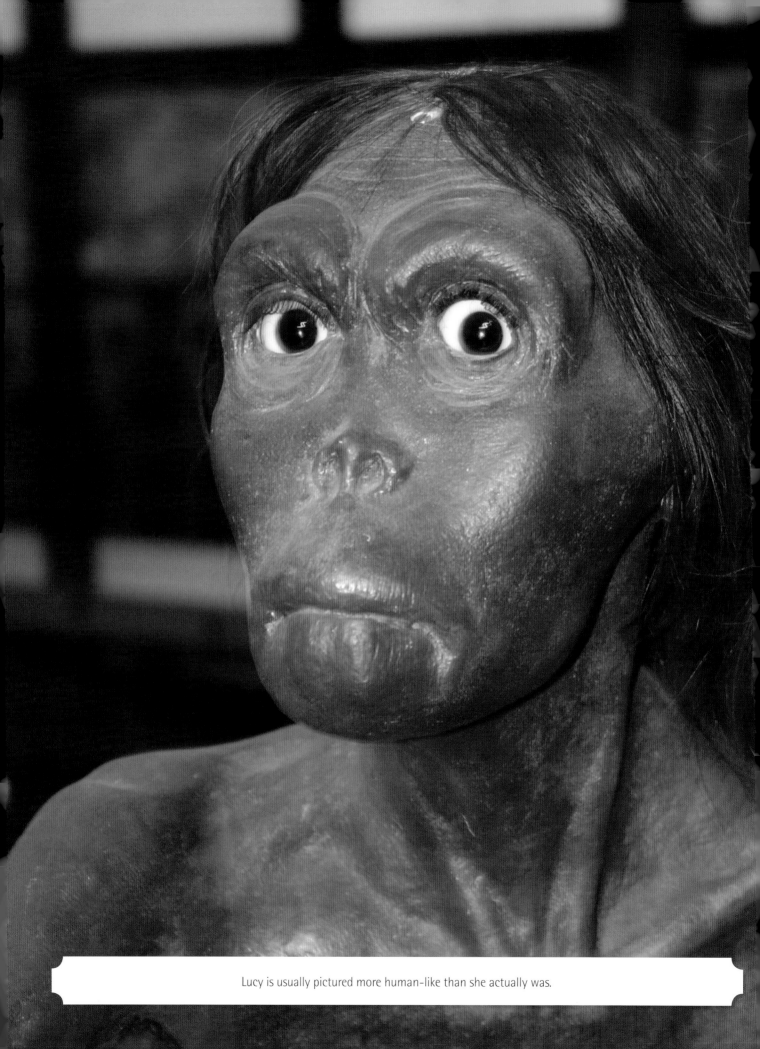

Lucy is usually pictured more human-like than she actually was.

WHAT ARE THEY, REALLY?

Ardipithecus

This genus is composed of a group of extinct apes.

Australopithecines

This is a group of extinct apes. Although often portrayed otherwise, australopithecines had obviously ape skulls, pelvises, hands, and feet.

Australopithecus afarensis (Lucy)

Paleoanthropologists Jack Stern and Randall Sussman have reported that Lucy's hands are "surprisingly similar to hands found in the small end of the pygmy chimpanzee-common chimpanzee range." They report that the feet, like the hands, are "long, curved and heavily muscled" much like those of living tree-dwelling primates. The authors conclude that no living primate has such hands and feet "for any purpose other than to meet the demands of full or part-time arboreal (tree-dwelling) life." (*American Journal of Physical Anthropology* **60**, 1983, pp. 279–317.)

A more recent report concludes that the australopithecine jaw closely resembles that of a gorilla. See www.answersingenesis.org/articles/2007/04/18/farewell-lucy.

Cro-Magnon

Far from being "primitive," Cro-Magnons were early relatives of ours, fully human. Living sometime after the dispersion at Babel, this group of people knew how to build huts, make stone paving floors, construct kilns, and bake pottery. They made tools out of bone, flint, ivory, antler, and wood. They knew how to carve flutes of bone, make jewelry, and sew clothing. Their artwork (cave murals) was "worthy of a place among the masterpieces of world art" (*Encyclopedia Britannica*, 15th ed., volume 5, p. 291).

Homo erectus

This was a group of our ancestors who used stone tools, made fire, buried their dead, carved rock into figurines, built shelters, and even used watercraft. Of this taxon, Professor Marvin Lubenow (who has studied the claims regarding human evolution for 30 years) writes:

> When we compare the crania of *Homo erectus* with those of early *Homo sapiens* and Neanderthal, the similarities are striking. My own conclusion is that *Homo erectus* and Neanderthal are actually the same: *Homo erectus* is on the lower end, with regard to size, of a continuum that

includes *Homo erectus*, early *Homo sapiens*, and Neanderthal. (Bones of Contention, Grand Rapids: Baker, 2004, 2nd edition, p. 127.)

Homo ergaster

This was a name suggested for some East African *Homo erectus* fossils.

Laetoli footprints

These footprints, although linked with the australopithecines, actually belong to a human. According to evolutionist R.H. Tuttle:

> Strictly on the basis of the morphology of the G prints [prints found at a site labelled "G"], their makers could be classified as *Homo sp.* because they are so similar to those of *Homo sapiens*, but their early date would probably deter many paleoanthropologists from accepting this assignment. I suspect that if the prints were undated, or if they had been given younger dates, most experts would probably accept them as having been made by *Homo* ... .

> If the prints were produced by a small species of *Australopithecus* (southern ape) then we must conclude that it had virtually human feet which ... were used in a manner indistinguishable from those of slowly walking humans. ... The feet that produced the G trails are in no discernible features transitional between the feet of apes ... and those of *Homo sapiens*. They are like small barefoot *Homo sapiens*. (M.D. Leakey and J.M. Harris, eds., LAETOLI—*A Pliocene site in Northern Tanzania*. London: Clarendon Press, 1987, pp. 503–523.)

Homo habilis

This is an invalid taxon composed of a mixture of several species, with most of the fossils belonging to australopithecines, according to Professor Marvin Lubenow (see www.answersingenesis.org/docs2006/0417ethiopian.asp).

Neanderthal

Neanderthals were fully human. According to Neanderthal authority Erik Trinkaus:

> Detailed comparisons of Neanderthal skeletal remains with those of modern humans have shown that there is nothing in Neanderthal anatomy that conclusively indicates locomotor, manipulative, intellectual, or linguistic abilities inferior to those of modern humans. (E. Trinkaus, "Hard Times Among the Neanderthals," *Natural History* **87**:10, p. 58.)

For more information, see www.answersingenesis.org/articles/am/v1/n2/worthy-ancestors and www.answersingenesis.org/articles/am/v2/n1/worthy-ancestors-2.

CAVEMEN?

Some museum dioramas may feature stooped, brutish, unkempt humans living in caves—primitive, subhuman cavemen.

In fact, people throughout history have lived in caves, and some even live in caves today. This does not mean that cave-people were (or are!) in any way more primitive than modern humans. It simply means that they were people who chose to live in caves (or were forced to live in caves because of extenuating circumstances).

After the people were scattered from Babel, some may have sought temporary shelter in caves, while working on building more permanent shelters for themselves. Additionally, Lot (Genesis 19:30), David (1 Samuel 22:1–24:7), and Elijah (1 Kings 19:9–13) at one time or another called a cave their home. Obadiah hid prophets in a cave (1 Kings 18:4), and the Israelites (Judges 6:2) escaped the Midianites by living in caves. Also, the Essenes, a Jewish sect living shortly before and after the time of Christ, lived and had libraries in caves. The discovered copies of many of their scrolls of Scripture and other Jewish literature are now known as the Dead Sea Scrolls.

For more information, see www.answersingenesis.org/creation/v26/i1/malta.asp.

A sculpture of Saint George defeating the dragon.
Mankind has been working with metals almost since the beginning of time.

STONES, BRONZE, IRON

Many museums feature depictions of prehistoric man in various settings, using various types of tools. Allegedly, the more primitive people used tools of stone, progressed to making tools of bronze, and culminated with making tools of iron.

However, from the Bible, we know that almost from the beginning, men were working with metals, and, thus, making tools of iron. The great-great-great-great-great grandson of Adam was Tubal-Cain, who was an "instructor of every craftsman in bronze and iron" (Genesis 4:22). And Noah must have used various types of tools to build his giant boat. Presumably, he would have passed his knowledge on to his sons, who taught their sons, and so on.

At Babel, the people quickly scattered. In rebuilding their lives elsewhere, some may have used the available materials—stones or wood—to fashion new homes. Later, they took more time to find ores and then smelt new metal tools and build other homes for themselves. Other family groups may have simply lacked the knowledge of how to work with metal, and only used what was nearby in their tool-making.

In fact, scientists have found that the Haya people of Tanzania were making medium-carbon steel in preheated, forced-draft furnaces long before Europeans began steelwork in the nineteenth century. For more information, see www.answersingenesis.org/creation/v2/i1/steel.asp.

Stone carvings such as these provide us with glimpses into the lives
of those who settled around the world after leaving Babel.

WHAT ABOUT THOSE DATES?

When looking at human artifacts dated 10,000 BC, or reading about the history of the Aborigines from 40,000 BC, keep in mind that these "ages" are based on many assumptions. In some cases, the ages stem from a dating method known as "Carbon-14." However, as shown elsewhere (see pages 165–167), radioisotope methods do not yield reliable results without being properly interpreted.

In other instances, the dates given result from a civilization's chronology of the past (for example, the Sumerian King List, China's dynasty and emperor list, Egypt's list of pharaohs). Again, historians have made many assumptions about these chronologies (for example, assuming that leaders never ruled at the same time), yielding greatly inflated dates. However, as historians and archaeologists continue to study these lists, they have realized that the ages of the civilizations should be reduced, bringing them in line with a biblical timeframe.

As you read about these dates, keep the following Bible-based timeline in mind.

4004 BC	The first humans were created.
2348 BC	Noah and his family were the only survivors of the global Flood. Because of the worldwide destruction of the Flood, we wouldn't expect to find much, if any, archaeological evidence from before this time.
ca. 2247 BC	The people began to disperse from the plain of Shinar (located in present-day Iraq).
2234 BC	Babylon begins.
2188 BC	Egypt is founded by Mizraim, son of Ham. It was after this time that the pyramids were built.
2089 BC	Greece begins.

For more information, visit www.answersingenesis.org/go/history.

No matter what ethnic group we're from, all humans are descendants of Adam and Eve, and thus all related.

THE ORIGIN OF THE PEOPLE GROUPS

Genesis 10 gives us a list of the names of the grandsons of Noah. The descendants of these families later traveled to other parts of the world via land bridges (that existed as a result of the Ice Age) to the Americas or Australia or on boats to the Pacific Islands, for example.

Gomer   His descendants settled in Galatia in modern Turkey. From there, they migrated to France, Spain, Wales, Germany, and Armenia. He was also the father of the Miautso people of China.

Magog   His descendants (the Scythians) inhabited parts of Romania and the Ukraine. He was also the ancestor of the Goths. The Irish Celts also trace their ancestry to him.

Madai   His descendants were the Medes. The Medes and Persians are the ancestors of those who live in Iran. The Medes also traveled into India.

Javan   He was the father of the Greek people. His children also settled in Cilicia and Cyprus. His later descendants gave rise to many of the European nations, including the Britons.

Tubal   His descendants became known as Iberes, and they settled in Georgia (in the former Soviet Union).

Meshech   Moscow and the surrounding region were settled by Meshech.

Tiras   His descendants were called Thracians, and they settled much of what is known as Yugoslavia.

Cush   The Ethiopians came from the line of Cush.

Mizraim   He and his family traveled to and settled in Egypt.

Phut   Phut founded Libya.

Canaan   He founded Palestine (modern Israel and Jordan). His children were Philistim (Philistines), Sidon, Heth (Hittites, Jebusites, Amorites, Girgasites, Hivites, Arkites, Sinites, Arvadites, Zemarites, Hamathites), Nimrod (founded Bablyon in 2234 BC), Erech, Accad, and Calneh.

Elam   He founded Persia. His descendants eventually merged with the Medes to form the nation of Iran.

Asshur   His descendants became known as the Assyrians.

Arphaxad   He and his family founded Chaldea. Eber gave rise to the Hebrew nation. Joktan's sons settled Arabia.

Lud   Lud gave rise to the Lydians (Western Turkey).

Aram   He settled the area known as Syria. His people are called the Arameans, and they speak Aramaic (a language that Jesus spoke while He was here on earth).

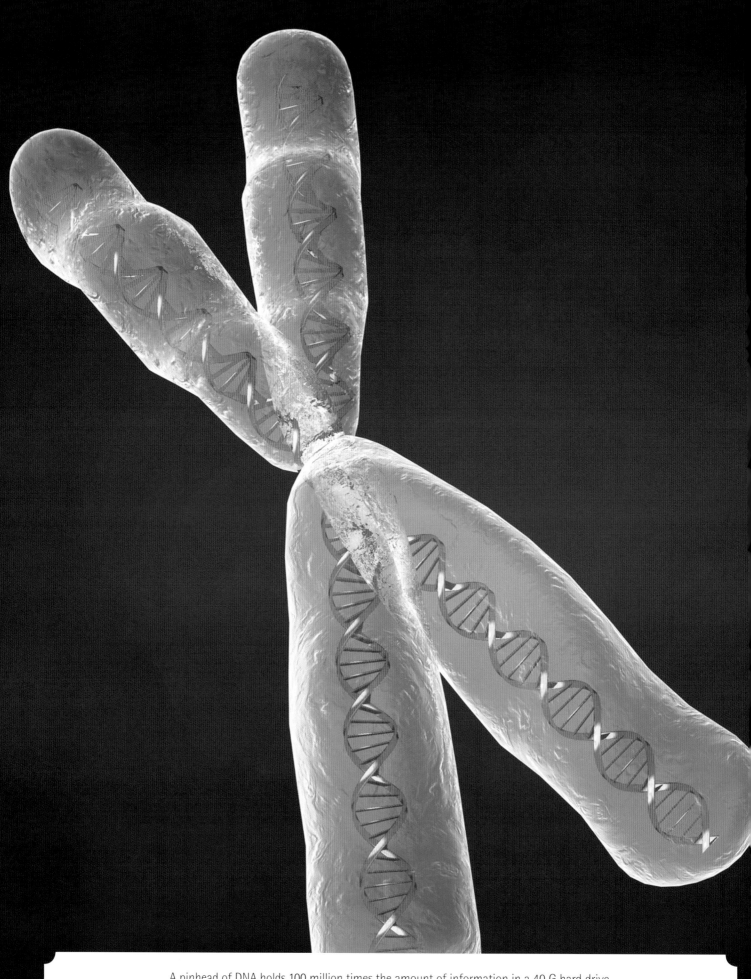

A pinhead of DNA holds 100 million times the amount of information in a 40 G hard drive.

HOW SIMILAR IS OUR DNA?

Some newer museum exhibits have begun to cite genetic "evidence" that humans and chimps are related. Molecular geneticist Dr. Georgia Purdom discusses the alleged DNA similarities:

When studying the human genome and its similarity to that of the chimp, scientists have recently concluded that 96% of our genome is similar. However, most people are unaware that this percent pertains to the regions of our DNA that result in proteins. It seems logical that if a protein performs a certain function in one organism, then that same protein should perform the same function in a variety of organisms. This is evidence for a common designer as much as for a common ancestor.

But most of the DNA sequence performs an unknown function and has been largely dismissed as "junk DNA." However, increasing evidence supports the view that "junk" DNA performs an important role. For example, a recent report unexpectedly found specific sequence patterns in "junk" DNA which scientists have termed "pyknons." It has been suggested that these pyknons may be important in determining when and where proteins are made.

Within this "junk DNA" there may be large differences between man and chimp. The areas of greatest difference appear to involve regions which are structurally different (commonly called "rearrangements") and areas of heterochromatin (tightly packed DNA).

She adds the following points:
- The chimp genome is 12% larger than the human genome.
- Several hundred million bases (individual components of the DNA) of the chimp genome are still unanalyzed.
- In many areas of the genome, major "rearrangements" of DNA sequences seem apparent, accounting for another 4–10% dissimilarity.
- Chimps have 23 chromosome pairs and humans have 22 chromosome pairs (excluding sex chromosomes for both species).

(Georgia Purdom, "If human and chimp DNA are so similar, why are there so many physical and mental differences between them?" online at www.answersingenesis.org/articles/am/v1/n2/human-and-chimp-dna.)

Then God said: "Let the earth bring forth grass, the herb that yields seed, and the fruit tree that yields fruit according to its kind." Gen. 1:11

III

PLANT EXHIBITS

Originally, plants were the only source of food for Adam, Eve, and the animals.

ARE PLANTS "ALIVE"?

Plants grow and reproduce, and many scientists consider plants "alive" in the biological sense.

However, according to the Word of God, there is a significant difference between plant "life," on the one hand, and animal and human life, on the other hand. Throughout the Bible, the Hebrew words *nephesh chayyâh* are used to describe human and animal life (e.g., Genesis 1:20–21, 24, 30; 27). When referring to mankind, *nephesh chayyâh* means "living soul" or "soulish creature," and when it refers to animals, it means "living creature." However, these words are never applied to plant life. There is a plain distinction.

God created all of the original plant kinds on Day 3 of Creation Week (Genesis 1:11). As you walk through the exhibits that feature different types of vegetation, look for plant features that are beneficial to humans. Although their medicinal properties would not have been needed before the Fall, plants were the only source of food for Adam and Eve while they were in the Garden of Eden (Genesis 1:29–30).

For more information, visit www.answersingenesis.org/articles/am/v1/n2/do-leaves-die.

God created the plants to reproduce "after their kind," which is what we observe happening today.

PLANT "EVOLUTION"?

The virtual tour page of the Smithsonian Museum of Natural History's fossil plants section states:

> Before plants, the surface of the early Earth was barren rock. In these halls, you can follow 410 million years of plant evolution, as plants developed new reproductive strategies for dealing with the varied and often extreme conditions on land. Early land plants reproduced by spores, like ferns do today. Then, about 340 million years ago, these pioneers gave rise to seed-bearing plants. Plant evolution took another leap 125 million years ago when flowering plants appeared. (www.mnh.si.edu/museum/VirtualTour/Tour/First/FossilPlants/index.html)

Evolutionists generally agree that plants evolved from algae that slowly began to colonize the land. This transition would need to involve the development of several key systems including those which prevent drying out in the air, absorb nutrients from the soil, enable the plant to grow upright without the support of water, and allow the plant to reproduce on land. However, these features require the addition of huge amounts of new genetic information—a process that hasn't been observed.

Along with these new information-gaining changes, many intricate symbiotic relationships supposedly developed. Many exclusive symbiotic relationships exist between fungi, bacteria, and insects. If these relationships are disturbed, the plants either do not survive or are less able to compete.

Additionally, within the evolutionary worldview, there are no known ancestors for most of the major plant phyla.

Remember, God created the various kinds of plants on Day 3 (Genesis 1:11), before He created the sun, moon, sea creatures, or land animals.

Harvard-trained paleontologist Dr. Kurt Wise believes the fossil record of plants reflects the order in which a pre-Flood floating forest was buried. For more information on his theory, see K. Wise, "The Pre-Flood Floating Forest," *Proceedings of the Fifth International Conference on Creationism*, Creation Science Fellowship, 2003, pp. 371–381.

Plants are able to transform sunlight, carbon dioxide, and water into energy in a marvelous process called photosynthesis.

THE ORIGIN OF PHOTOSYNTHESIS

Plants are able to transform sunlight, carbon dioxide, and water into energy in a marvelous process called photosynthesis.

There are many problems with the naturalistic origin of photosynthesis. For example, 17 enzymes are required to assemble chlorophyll. Without each of these 17 enzymes, photosynthesis cannot happen. Where did the information come from in the first place that tells these enzymes how to combine to form chlorophyll? Evolutionists have never explained, much less proven, what they imagine to have happened.

Additionally, the intermediate products resulting from photosynthesis are toxic to the cell. Without the proper enzymes being present at the same time to detoxify the process, photosynthesis would kill the cell that was photosynthesizing. The low probability of all the enzymes evolving simultaneously makes it virtually impossible that photosynthesis occurred by chance in "primitive" bacteria, as protozoa-to-plants evolution claims.

From a biblical perspective, we understand that God created the various plant kinds with the ability to photosynthesize from the beginning.

For more information, see www.answersingenesis.org/tj/v17/i3/photosynthesis.asp.

The oldest living trees began growing after the floodwater retreated, 4,300 years ago.

HOW OLD ARE THE TREES?

When considering the information we can glean from trees concerning the age of the earth, keep in mind that 4,300 years ago, the Genesis Flood disrupted the surface of the earth—and everything growing on it. It's highly unlikely that any vegetation (other than seeds, spores, and floating mats of vegetation) would have survived this watery catastrophe. So, any age estimates need to fit within this framework.

Scientists have acquired "ages" from trees in several ways.

Rings

Rather than growing only annual rings, trees are now known to produce more than one ring per year under certain conditions. In some trees, 3–5 rings per year have been documented, while certain pines have been shown to produce 2–6 rings per year. (J. Woodmorappe, "Collapsing the Long Bristlecone Pine Tree Ring Chronologies," *Proceedings of the Fifth International Conference on Creationism*. Creation Science Fellowship, 2003, pp. 491–503)

Cross-matching

In some cases, scientists compare rings of different trees (for instance, bristlecone pines), attempting to correlate growth rings. These comparisons have yielded a record of 8,000+ years.

However, several factors can affect the correlation. For example, earthquakes, soil conditions, insect infestations, and atmospheric conditions (e.g., high volumes of CO_2) could cause some bristlecones to show different growth rings from others growing at the same time. When these factors, along with other assumptions, are taken into consideration, the "ages" of these trees fall by at least half, bringing them in line with a biblical timeframe. (J. Woodmorappe, "Collapsing the Long Bristlecone Pine Tree Ring Chronologies," *Proceedings of the Fifth International Conference on Creationism*. Creation Science Fellowship, 2003, pp. 491–503.)

From a biblical perspective, we would expect all life to be interconnected to some degree, since it was all brought into being by the Creator God.

WEB OF LIFE EXHIBITS

After Adam's sin, many animals developed carnivorous tastes and eventually the present-day "food chain" developed.

FOOD CHAIN FROM THE BEGINNING?

In many ways, living things and plants are dependent on each other. Many museums use this concept to suggest that things have evolved to fill a certain niche. We depend on plants for food and oxygen; plants need the carbon dioxide we breathe out. Some species exhibit complex symbiotic relationships, without which they wouldn't survive. No living thing exists in a complete vacuum.

From a biblical perspective, we would expect all of life to be interconnected to some degree. In the beginning, God created plants for us and the animals to eat. His completed original world was perfectly capable of continuing to thrive. However, Adam's sin corrupted the original perfection of the world.

The Curse God placed on His creation (Genesis 3:14–19, cf. Romans 8:19–23) introduced new dynamics into the world. It was after this time that many animals became carnivorous. Eventually the present-day "food chain" developed. However, this is not upward evolution. Rather it is a downward "devolution" from the original order of things.

We can marvel at the symbiotic relationships that don't involve the death of *nephesh* creatures. However, we need to keep in mind that this world is not the one that God originally created—it is a fallen, cursed version. We still see abundant evidence of God's creative genius, power, and handiwork. But we also see evidence of His righteous judgments at the Fall and the Flood. And in some cases, we get glimpses of the original non-carnivorous creation (and the one to which it will eventually be restored). For example, pigs and tigers live together in harmony in a zoo in Thailand. In another situation, a lioness grew up refusing to eat meat. (D. Catchpoole, "Tigers and pigs ... together?" *Creation* **27**:3, June 2005, pp. 28–29, online at www.answersingenesis.org/creation/v27/i3/together.asp, and D. Catchpoole, "The lion that wouldn't eat meat," *Creation* **22**:2, March 2000, pp. 22–23, online at www.answersingenesis.org/creation/v22/i2/lion.asp.)

For more information, see www.answersingenesis.org/go/curse.asp.

The intricate design seen throughout nature testifies to the Creator.

125

OTHER "EVIDENCE FOR EVOLUTION" EXHIBITS

Was the dingo present in the Garden of Eden? No, this animal is a descendant of the original dog "kind."

DOES SPECIATION = EVOLUTION?

Some museums show their lack of understanding of the biblical position when they claim that creationists believe in the "fixity of species," that is, that all animals have remained unchanged since the beginning. However, this does *not* represent the creationist position.

We freely admit (based on information gleaned from the Bible) that God created the original animal and plant kinds with great genetic variation and that descendants of those original created kinds can vary greatly within their kind.

In most cases, a kind represents a group of animals that can mate with others in that group. It appears from ongoing creationist research that the created "kinds" were much larger genetic categories than the "species" designation that scientists use today. Except for mankind, each created kind was at the genus or even family level (perhaps higher in some cases) of modern taxonomic classification.

For example, lions, tigers, jaguars, and leopards are classified as different species, but are probably all members of an original cat kind. And donkeys, zebras, Thoroughbreds, and Arabian horses are probably all part of the original horse kind. Some have suggested that there may have been as few as 50 different dinosaur kinds (compared to the over 1,000 species and 500 genera that the evolutionists classify). For example, the ceratopsian kind might include triceratops, monoceratops, etc.

The representatives of each kind that survived the Flood had enough information in their DNA to produce the wide variety of animals that we see today. The varieties that we only see preserved in the fossil record came from the genetic potential in the DNA of the original created kinds.

After erecting the false view, the museums may then proceed to knock down the "fixity of species" argument by showing that animals change over time, and that new species have been observed to arise. This, they claim, is evidence for molecules-to-man evolution. For example, the exhibits may feature varieties of weasels, rabbits, dogs, and cats. The signage then points out, "See, animals change. That's evolution."

When museums use evolution to mean both "change in features over time" and "the history of life on earth," this is an example of equivocation or "bait-and-switch." They are using examples of variation *within* one of the created kinds (as evidenced by a new species arising, for example) as proof of microbe-to-microbiologist change *between* different kinds.

Speciation can be defined as "the process of change in a population that produces distinct populations which rarely interbreed in nature due to geographic isolation or other factors." This observable process (which, incidentally has been shown to happen much faster than evolutionists expected) fits into the category of operational science (not origins science). All informed creationists accept speciation as a fact of nature, but contend that this process cannot explain goo-to-you-via-the-zoo evolution.

The formation of a new species generally results in a loss of genetic information—the opposite type of change required by molecules-to-man evolution. As two populations of the same created kind become separated, genetic variation is diminished, resulting in the formation of a new species. But speciation has never been observed to turn one kind of animal into another kind. There is a limit to the amount of change a population can produce.

When small changes that arise as a result of the loss of information are used as evidence for molecules-to-man evolution, the equivocating switch has occurred. Be on the lookout for when museums do this in their signage.

For more information, visit www.answersingenesis.org/go/speciation.

DO MUTATIONS FUEL EVOLUTION?

Some exhibits may present mutations as the fuel for particles-to-presidents evolutionary processes. The claim is that small changes in the genome can eventually result in one kind changing into a completely different kind of animal or plant, given enough time.

However, scientific observations have shown that virtually all mutations result in a loss in the information content of a genome, rather than the net gain that amoeba-to-archaeologist evolution requires. No mutation has been observed that causes an increase in (or new) genetic information.

As you ponder the exhibits about mutations, look for the answer to the question, "Where did all the new information come from since mutations are known to reduce or duplicate or reshuffle *existing* information?"

For more information, visit www.answersingenesis.org/go/mutations.

Some may wrongly point to sickle-cell anemia as an example of an advantageous mutation in malaria infested parts of the world.. However, even in this case, the mutation has resulted in a serious disease, and a loss of *already-existing* genetic information.

For more information on sickle-cell anemia, visit www.answersingenesis.org/creation/v16/i2/anaemia.asp.

Natural selection may bring about a new *species* of animal, but cannot generate a new *kind* of animal.

IS NATURAL SELECTION EVIDENCE FOR EVOLUTION?

You may encounter many examples of "natural selection in action" while visiting the museum. Many evolutionists claim that natural selection is the process that drives molecules-to-man evolution; however, evolution requires that, over time, living things must add more information to their DNA as they gain new features, abilities, or structures. Natural selection actually works in the *opposite* direction of what molecules-to-man evolution requires. It selects from *already-existing* genetic information, and cannot generate *new* genetic information.

God created the original animal kinds with much diversity in their DNA, so that as they reproduced and filled the earth, their descendants were able to adapt to many different environments. Scientists *have* observed this—animals reproduce "after their kind" (dogs have puppies, cats have kittens, geese have goslings, kangaroos have joeys, etc.).

The genetic makeup of some members of a kind is more suitable to certain environments. Natural selection is the process by which animals die out when they don't have the genetic makeup that allows them to survive in their environment.

Those animals that survive reproduce more animals like themselves. For example, many animals that live in drier regions of the world are able to gain most of the water they need from the plants they eat. Animals without this ability would have a harder time trying to survive in that region, and would eventually die out.

Natural selection may bring about a new *species* of animal, but it cannot generate a new *kind* of animal.

For more information, visit www.answersingenesis.org/go/selection.

Biblical creationists consider an animal's major structures to be part of the original design provided by God.

ARE ADAPTATIONS EVIDENCE FOR EVOLUTION?

Some museum exhibits may attempt to show that a given characteristic of an organism was produced through a gradual series of changes. For example, an exhibit may feature a fish fin turning into a tetrapod leg. This so-called transition is thought to be an adaptation that arose as a fish's fins adapted to crawling in a shallow stream, thus providing some form of advantage.

Adaptations can be defined as "physical traits or behaviors due to inherited characteristics that give organisms the ability to survive in a given environment." Biblical creationists consider major structures to be part of the original design provided by God. Modifications to those structures (adaptations) occur due to genetic recombination, and random mutations. These structures do not arise from the modification of similar structures of another kind of animal. As pointed out elsewhere, mutations and natural selection can only operate on existing genetic information—they cannot generate the copious amounts of new information required by evolutionary ideas (for example, the genetic information required to go from a fin to a leg).

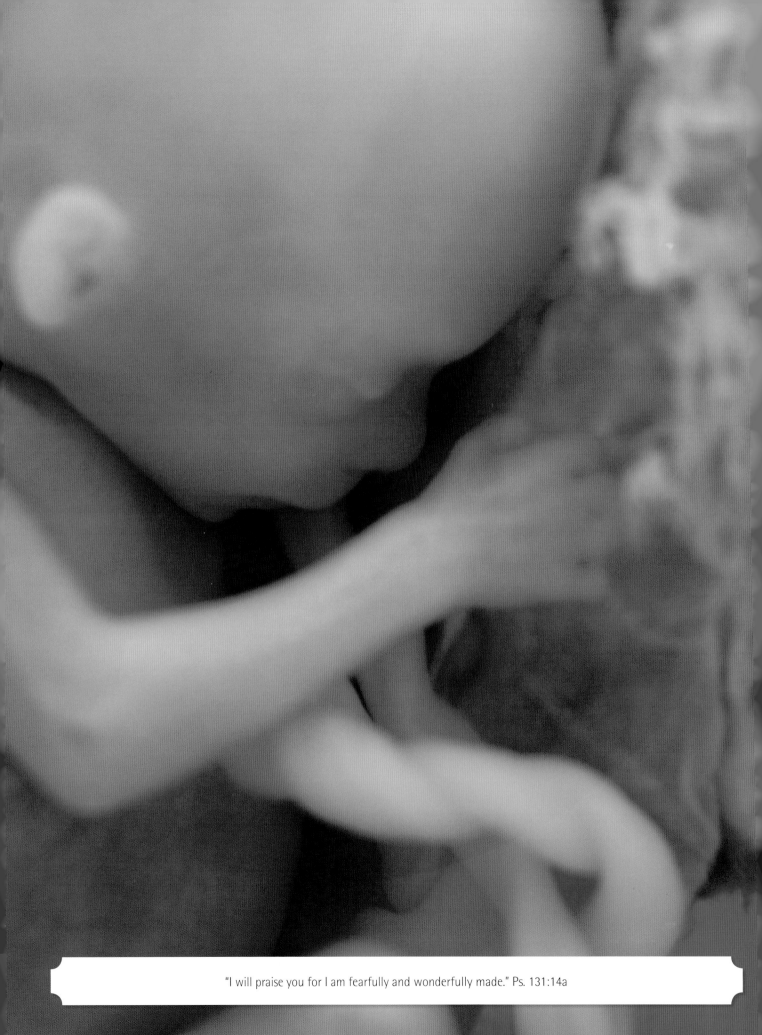

"I will praise you for I am fearfully and wonderfully made." Ps. 131:14a

WHAT ABOUT THOSE EMBRYOS?

Although most museums now recognize that the human embryo does not pass through various evolutionary stages (known as *embryonic recapitulation*, or the biogenetic law, which was based on fraudulent drawings by the nineteenth century German evolutionist, Ernst Haeckel), they may continue to cite *embryonic homology* as evidence of evolution. This is the idea that embryos look similar at early stages and is based on drawings published by Haeckel in 1866. The London Science Museum states on its website:

> The embryos of vertebrates (animals with backbones) pass through a common stage early in their development. At this stage they show strong similarities, although the animals come to be as different as a human and a cat. This happens as their body plans are being laid down. It seems that an efficient way of marking out the body plan arose millions of years ago, and has remained virtually unchanged throughout animal evolution. (www.sciencemuseum.org.uk/on-line/lifecycle/24.asp)

However, this idea of similarity is now known to be false. Evolutionist Michael Richardson experimentally showed in 1997 that embryos of various creatures do not look the same (Michael Richardson. *et al.*, *Anatomy and Embryology*, 196:2, pp. 91–106). In fact, Haeckel's drawings were complete fabrications. Richardson stated:

> This is one of the worst cases of scientific fraud. It's shocking to find that somebody one thought was a great scientist was deliberately misleading. It makes me angry ... What he [Haeckel] did was to take a human embryo and copy it, pretending that the salamander and the pig and all the others looked the same at the same stage of development. They don't ... These are fakes. (Interview with Nigel Hawkes, *The Times*, London, August 11, 1997, p. 14)

Richardson found that Haeckel added, omitted, and changed features, and he also fudged the scale to exaggerate similarities among species, even when there were 10-fold differences in size. Haeckel further blurred differences by neglecting to name the species in most cases, as if one representative was accurate for an entire group of animals. (Elizabeth Pennisi, "Haeckel's Embryos: Fraud Rediscovered," *Science* **277**:5331, September 5, 1997, p. 1,435.) If the museum's illustrations are drawings, they are most likely based on Haeckel's fake drawings, which are completely out of touch with reality. However, if the museum's illustrations are actual photos, notice that the embryos really don't look alike.

For more information, see www.answersingenesis.org/creation/v20/i2/fraud.asp.

In what ways are humans similar to apes? In what ways are we different?

ARE SIMILARITIES EXPLAINED BY EVOLUTION?

As is obvious even from a quick glance at earth's fauna, there are many similarities among organisms. Bats, insects, birds, and pterodactyls all have wings. Cats, dinosaurs, cattle, and deer all have four legs. As new advances in science have come about, scientists have been able to compare animals on many levels—from the outward appearance to gene sequences.

Evolutionists have developed two ideas to explain the similarities that exist among living things.

Homology is the term used to describe structures in animals that are alike due to their supposed shared ancestry. Most museums include exhibits that discuss the homologous structures to show evolutionary relationships. For example, they may point to the seven neck vertebrae in humans and giraffes, or to the wings of bats and the arms of humans, or to the five-fingered design among most vertebrates as evidence that we share a common ancestor.

Analogy refers to structures that perform the same function by similar mechanisms in animals which are not thought to have a common ancestor. Many analogous structures are thought to be the result of *convergent evolution*, which is the separate evolution of similar structures in different animals because of similar environmental pressures.

With similarities to placentals, marsupials are thought to be an example of convergent evolution. *The Teacher's Guide to the Hall of Mammals* at the Smithsonian Museum of Natural History states of the marsupials in Australia, "The splendid isolation of the island continent has resulted in a uniquely fantastic evolution of mammals. Here evolution worked in isolation and yet often produced convergences of adaptations found in mammals inhabiting other continents."

However, the creationist Dr. Jerry Bergman explains homologies and analogies this way.

> The simplest and most obvious explanation for the fact that morphological similarities between bones, sensory organs, lungs, or gills exist among most higher animals is that the *requirements of life are similar* for similar living things, and some designs are preferred in constructing animals because these designs are superior to competing designs. (Jerry Bergman, "Does homology provide evidence of evolutionary naturalism?," *TJ* **15**:1, 2001, pp. 26–33, available online at www.answersingenesis. org/tj/v15/i1/homology.asp)

A COMMON ANCESTOR
ISN'T THE ANSWER

Recent findings from various scientific disciplines confirm that homology is not evidence that all living things share a common ancestor.

Embryology: From an evolutionary perspective, it would make sense that similar structures would develop similarly in the womb. However, many similar structures develop from different groups of embryonic cells. For example, the forelimbs of the newt, lizard, and human develop from different trunk segments. And the kidneys of fish and amphibia develop differently than the kidneys of reptiles and humans. (Jerry Bergman, "Does homology provide evidence of evolutionary naturalism?," *TJ* **15**:1, 2001, pp. 26–33, available online at www.answersingenesis.org/tj/v15/i1/homology.asp.)

Biochemistry: The similarity in the chemical make-up and function of cells in all living things is actually an argument *against* molecules-to-man evolution.

> But extensive biochemical research has revealed that the simplest reason for biochemical homology is that all life requires similar inorganic elements, compounds and biomolecules; consequently, all life is required to use similar metabolic pathways to process these compounds. Most organisms that use oxygen and rely on the metabolism of carbohydrates, fats and proteins must use a citric acid cycle which is remarkably similar in all organisms. Furthermore, the metabolism of most proteins into energy produces ammonia, which is processed for removal in similar ways in a **wide** variety of organisms. What evolutionists must explain is why billions of years of evolution have not produced major differences in the biochemistry of life.

> The problem for evolutionists is that the biochemistry of all life, even that allegedly separated by hundreds of millions of years of geologic time and evolution, *is too similar*. (Jerry Bergman, "Does homology provide evidence of evolutionary naturalism?," *TJ* **15**:1, 2001, pp. 26–33, available online at www.answersingenesis.org/tj/v15/i1/homology.asp.)

Genetics: Evolutionist Gavin De Beer is quoted as saying:

> Because homology implies community of descent from ... a common ancestor it might be thought that genetics would provide the key to the problem of homology. This is where the worst shock of all

is encountered ... [because] characters controlled by identical genes are not necessarily homologous ... [and] homologous structures need not be controlled by identical genes. (Jonathan Wells, *Icons of Evolution: Science or Myth? Why much of what we teach about evolution is wrong.* Washington: Regnery Publ., 2000, p. 73.)

Vestigial organs: In the early 1900s, evolutionists believed there were about 180 organs in the human body that had no function. They claimed these organs were evolutionary leftovers—evidence that we shared a common ancestor with all living things. According to evolutionists, organs that played a role in more primitive life forms were not necessary in humans.

However, this idea is now known to be false. Each alleged "vestigial" organ is known to have an important function, e.g., the appendix plays a vital role in the immune system, while the tailbone provides support for the muscles in the floor of the pelvis. For more information, see www.answersingenesis.org/home/area/faq/vestigialorgans.asp.

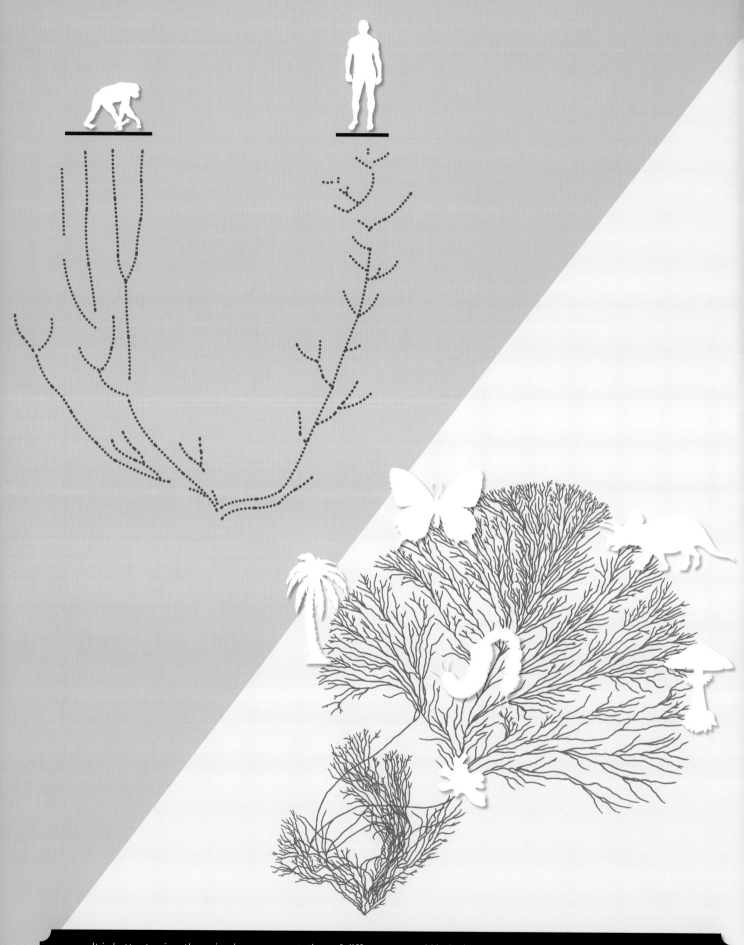

It is better to view the animals as representatives of different created kinds that were buried at various stages during the Flood (or in post-Flood localized catastrophes), rather than as a showcase of onward-upward evolution.

HOW TO READ A "FAMILY TREE"

Most museums feature charts that illustrate the alleged evolutionary lineage of the animal in question—birds, dinosaurs, reptiles, humans, etc. These "family trees" are supposed to show how the group of organisms has developed (evolved) over time from a common ancestor. These charts have been constructed based on fossil evidence, although more recently DNA and molecular studies have come into play.

In a fascinatingly frank observation, one evolutionist admits the truth about the fossil record and the evolutionary relationships that have been built on it:

> Remember that although a living individual must have had ancestors, fossils are unlikely to represent any of them. Even if a fossil was an ancestor, we will never know this—we can never know with certainty what happened in the past. Accepting that fossils are not ancestors also means that there are no "missing links" in the fossil record because fossils cannot be ordered, as traditionally depicted, into an evolutionary lineage. There is no ladder of life. Most, if not all, fossils lie on the dead branches of the tree of life, and we must remember that most of our tree of life is dead, with only a few green living leaves at the tips of the branches. (D.M. Irwin, "Dead branches on the tree of life," *Nature* **403**, 2000, p, 480.)

Remember, fossils don't speak for themselves; they must be interpreted. The lines leading to the various branches on the tree represent the interpretation. The actual fossil evidence is usually pictured at the end of the branches.

When viewing a family tree, it's helpful to disregard the lines (dotted or otherwise) leading to animals. If the museum has any honesty at all, the actual fossil evidence will be shown in bars or different colored lines compared to the imaginary branches. Once these imaginary interpretations of the evidence are eliminated, it becomes much easier to view the animals as representatives of different created kinds that were buried at various stages during the Flood (or in post-Flood localized catastrophes), rather than as a showcase of onward-upward evolution.

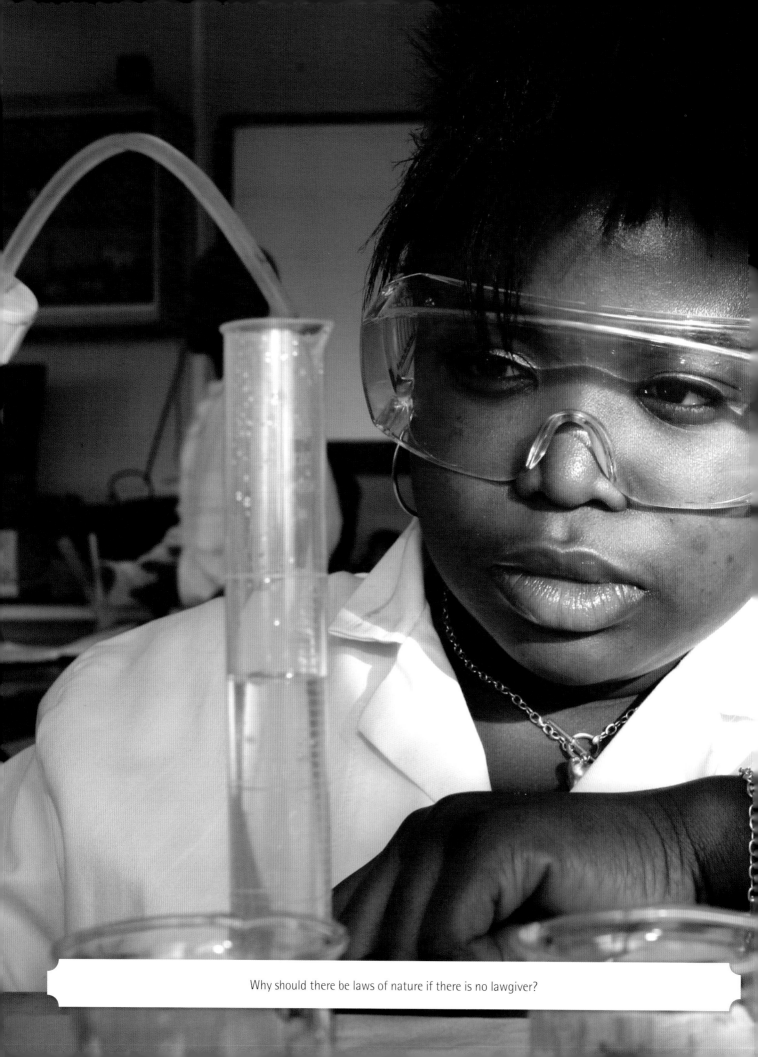

Why should there be laws of nature if there is no lawgiver?

HOW IMPORTANT IS EVOLUTION TO SCIENCE?

Some museum exhibits may claim that evolution is the foundation to all of science. Those who deny evolution may be compared to those who deny the well-established theory of gravity.

However, this "apples and alligators" comparison conveniently ignores the fact that gravity is a phenomenon that can be directly observed by experimentation, whereas particles-to-people evolution occurring over millions of years falls outside the domain of such inquiry. It is a story about the unobserved past.

Additionally, evolution is *not* foundational to modern science. Dr. Marc Kirschner, a prominent evolutionist, likes to invoke the much-quoted declaration of famed twentieth-century biologist Theodesius Dobzhansky that "nothing in biology makes sense except in the light of evolution" (the title of a 1973 essay). In reply, Kirschner points out that the evidence is quite to the contrary:

> In fact, over the last 100 years, almost all of biology has proceeded independent of evolution, except evolutionary biology itself. Molecular biology, biochemistry and physiology, have not taken evolution into account at all. (Marc Kirschner, quoted in Peter Dizikes, Missing Links," *Boston Globe*, October 23, 2005, www.boston.com/news/globe/ideas/articles/2005/10/23/missing_links/.)

Furthermore, Dr. Jason Lisle, a creationist astrophysicist, makes this significant observation:

> It is because a logical God created and ordered the universe that I, and other creationists, expect to be able to understand aspects of that universe through logic, careful observation and experimentation.

> Why should there be laws of nature if there is no lawgiver? If our minds have been designed, and if the universe has been constructed by God, as the Bible teaches, then of course we should be able to study nature. Science is possible because the Bible is true.

The great founders of science knew this to be true and based their work on their knowledge that God was the Creator. Isaac Newton, Blaise Pascal, James Joule, Louis Pasteur, Robert Boyle, and Johann Kepler (to name but a few) accepted the Bible as the Word of God and used it as the foundation for their scientific work.

The earth is actually three days older than the sun and moon!

HALL OF OUR EXCITING EARTH

In the beginning, God created the earth three days before He created the sun. Rather than being several billion years younger than the rest of the universe, as the evolutionary worldview claims, the earth is actually *older* than the sun, moon, and stars.

This section of the guide deals with exhibits of the many geophysical features of our earth—rock layers, fossils, plate tectonics, etc. It also deals with the various dating methods, pointing out problems with the billions-of-years ages that some methods yield. As you learn from these exhibits, remember that the Flood of Noah's day (and its continuing aftereffects) played a dramatic role in shaping the surface of the earth.

This is an artist's rendition of what the first continent, Rodinia, may have looked like.

THE EARLY EARTH
EXHIBITS

Stromatolites are finely layered accumulations of sediment bound by microorganisms, especially cyanobacteria.

A WORLD WITHOUT OXYGEN?

According to the American Museum of Natural History:

> Evidence of the evolution of Earth's atmosphere is given by a 2.7-billion-year-old specimen of a banded iron formation from Ontario, Canada. As single-celled organisms began generating oxygen through photosynthesis, iron and silica minerals in brilliant shades of red precipitated out of the oceans. The iron bands stopped forming once the atmosphere and ocean were saturated with oxygen, roughly 1.7 billion years ago. Other examples of this nascent period include stromatolites, fossil rocks from West Africa which were formed by blue-green algae some 900 million years ago. (www.amnh.org/rose/hope/evolved/)

However, scientists have now discovered that the earth's atmosphere has never been without oxygen (as we would expect since God created the world to be inhabited by animals and humans, Genesis 1).

Banded Iron Formations (BIFs)

Michael Oard suggests that the banded iron formations, allegedly evidence of the early earth atmosphere, are actually the result of the initial stages of the Flood. He speculates that BIFs could have formed quickly from the hot water and magma flows that resulted as the fountains of the great deep broke open.

Rapid currents then spread out from the eruptions, forming the BIFs. (M. Oard, "Could BIFs be caused by the fountains of the great deep?" *TJ* **11**:3, 1997, pp. 261–262) BIFs may also be pre-Flood hydrothermal deposits.

Stromatolites

Stromatolites are finely layered accumulations of sediment bound by microorganisms, especially cyanobacteria. They have a variety of forms including flat, sheet-like layers to large domal mounds.

Living stromatolites have been found in a variety of environments including desert streams, beneath frozen Antarctic lakes, freshwater African lakes, and marine settings. The most famous living examples are large dome-like stromatolites from the coast of Western Australia.

Fossil stromatolites are well known and occur throughout the fossil record, primarily in the Precambrian. Creationist opinions about their origin vary. Recently, Dr. Kurt Wise reported what he thought were stromatolites that grew in place in the Precambrian sediments (pre-Flood) of the Grand Canyon as part of a large hydrothermal system. (K. Wise, "The Hydrothermal Biome: a Pre-Flood Environment," *Proceedings of the Fifth International Conference on Creationism*. Creation Science Fellowhip, 2003, pp. 359–370.)

Dr. John Whitmore believes the fossil stromatolites of the Eocene Green River Formation represent stromatolites that grew in place after the Flood. (J. Whitmore, "The Green River Formation: a large post-Flood lake system, *Journal of Creation* **20**:1, 2006, pp. 55–63.)

More creationist work needs to be completed on the origin of other stromatolites in other parts of the fossil record before firm conclusions can be reached.

A HOT MOLTEN BLOB?

According to the American Museum of Natural History, "the planet took shape around a molten iron core" (www.amnh.org/rose/hope/evolved/).

Most museums picture the early earth as a hot molten blob. However, we know from the Bible that God formed the world covered with water. He created lush vegetation shortly thereafter and filled the world with living things over the following days.

Why are the landmasses the way they are?

MOVING CONTINENTS EXHIBITS

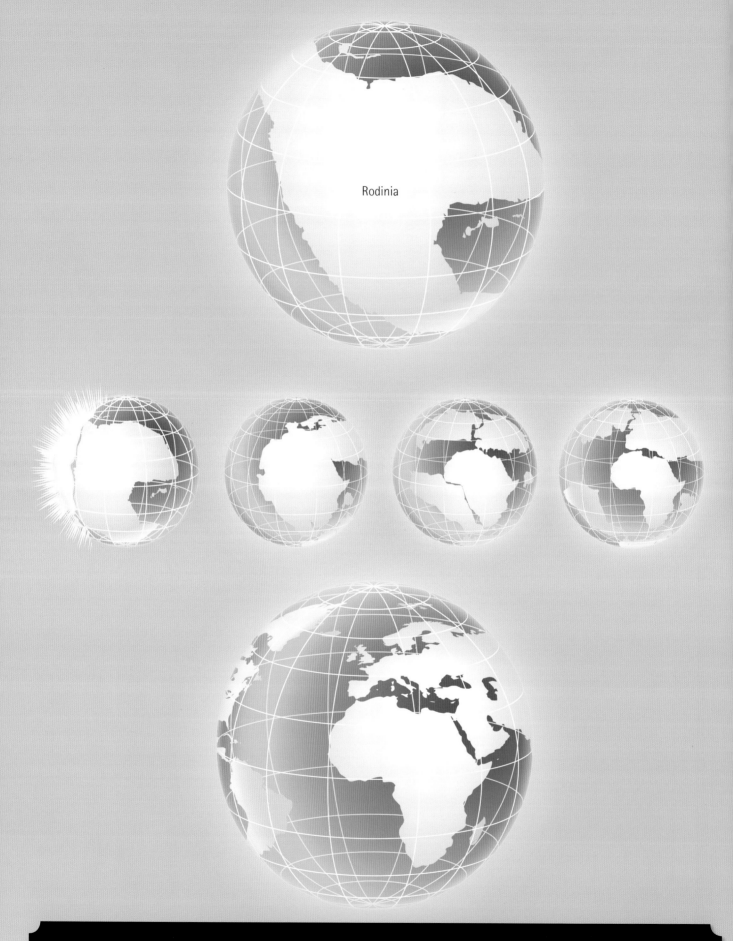

Rodinia

Some believe that Rodinia transitioned into today's continents during the year-long Flood of Noah's day.

PAST SUPERCONTINENTS

Some creationists have presented this model of how the earth's continents may have looked in the past.

Rodinia
Most secular and biblical geologists believe that all the land has been together more than once. One of these supercontinents is called "Rodinia" (from the Russian word for "motherland").

When God spoke the dry land into existence on Day 3 of Creation Week (Genesis 1:9–10), He may have created a landmass similar to Rodinia (scientists continue to debate its exact shape).

Dr. Kurt Wise believes that much of the area of the pre-Flood continents was covered in shallow oceans where invertebrate animals lived. A hot-water reef was located at the edge of the continents, while sand dunes were found along the beaches. (K. Wise, "The Hydrothermal Biome: a Pre-Flood Environment," *Proceedings of the Fifth International Conference on Creationism.* Creation Science Fellowhip, 2003, pp. 359–370.)

Pangaea
The Flood began with a breakup of the "fountains of the great deep" and an opening of the "windows of heaven" (Genesis 7:11). This may have been the result of the breakup of the original supercontinent into huge plates of the earth's crust. These plates split, moved, and collided throughout the duration of the Flood.

Evidence suggests that, after the breakup, the land again smashed together, forming another supercontinent called Pangaea. This temporary supercontinent formed and broke up entirely during the Flood.

Laurasia and Gondwana
Still during the Flood, Pangaea broke apart, first into Laurasia and Gondwana and finally into the continents we have today. At the end of this period, the Indian subcontinent slammed into the Eurasian plate, forming the Himalayas.

Most creationists believe the continents have moved, but not as slowly as the evolutionists claim.

HAVE THE CONTINENTS MOVED?

Yes, most creationists believe the continents have moved, although not as slowly as the museum exhibits may claim.

Dr. John Baumgardner has developed a model of "catastrophic plate tectonics" (see globalflood.org). According to the model, at the beginning of the Flood, thousands of miles of the earth's crust split apart along lines traversing the globe. The mantle rose to fill the voids between the splitting plates. When this 2,000°F (1,093°C) rock contacted the cool seawater above it, the seawater flashed into steam. This formed a line of steam jets along the boundaries of the plates (possibly the "fountains of the great deep").

The immense and incredibly powerful steam jets shot tens of thousands of feet into earth's atmosphere. Significant amounts of seawater were also lifted into the atmosphere. For several weeks, this fell to earth as intense global rain (possibly the "windows of heaven").

The rising of the mantle through earth's crust also resulted in a temporary rise in the global sea level, causing the oceans to flood the continents.

These simultaneous activities resulted in the dramatic shifting of the earth's crust to produce today's seven continents.

For more information, see www.answersingenesis.org/go/tectonics.

Most of today's mountain chains were formed during the Flood of Noah's day.

WHY ARE THERE OCEAN BASINS, CONTINENTS, AND MOUNTAINS?

Psalm 104 suggests an answer:

5 You who laid the foundations of the earth,

   So that it should not be moved forever,

6 You covered it with the deep as with a garment;

   The waters stood above the mountains.

7 At Your rebuke they fled;

   At the voice of Your thunder they hastened away.

8 They went up over the mountains;

   They went down into the valleys,

   To the place which You founded for them.

9 You have set a boundary that they may not pass over,

   That they may not return to cover the earth.

After the waters covered the mountains (verse 6), God rebuked them and they fled (verse 7); the mountains rose, the valleys sank down (verse 8), and God set a boundary so that they will never again cover the earth (verse 9; cf. Isaiah 54:9).

New continental landmasses bearing new mountain chains of folded rock strata were uplifted from below the globe-encircling waters that had eroded and leveled the pre-Flood topography, while large deep ocean basins were formed to receive and accommodate the Flood waters that then drained off the emerging continents.

That is why the oceans are so deep, and why there are folded mountain ranges.

In fact, fossilized sea creatures are found on top of the highest mountains on earth, showing that the layers forming the mountains were deposited under water during the Flood.

Canyons, such as this one, were formed by massive amounts of water over a short period of time.

WHEN DID CANYONS FORM?

In many museums, the story about canyon formation is that a river slowly and patiently carved the canyons over many thousands or millions of years.

Creation scientists believe that most of the world's canyons formed sometime after the Flood. The rock layers through which the canyons are carved were laid down during (or soon after) the global, watery catastrophe.

After the Flood, there would have been copious amounts of rainfall during the initial stages of the Ice Age. This rainfall created many lakes, which eventually breached their respective dams to form some of the canyons of the world. For example, some scientists believe that the Grand Canyon could have been carved in a relatively short amount of time when a massive amount of water in northeastern Arizona and Colorado catastrophically breached a dam and rushed out.

Additionally, there is now much evidence that some post-Flood flooding and canyon cutting occurred as a result of glacial outburst floods (or large amounts of water emanating from below ice sheets). For example, scientists believe that the Channeled Scablands were carved when Lake Missoula burst through its ice dam in northern Idaho and swept through eastern Washington into northern Oregon and out into the Pacific Ocean. They believe that the giant lake emptied in two days! For more information, visit www.answersingenesis.org/docs2003/1209missoula.asp.

There is much observational evidence that canyon formation can happen quickly. For example, Burlingame Canyon, near Walla Walla, Washington, was observed to form in less than six days in 1926! For more information, visit www.answersingenesis.org/creation/v24/i4/canyon.asp.

Creation scientists believe that many of the world's rock formations formed during and after the Flood.

ROCK EXHIBITS

Sedimentary rocks, such as these, do not contain atomic clocks.

HOW OLD ARE ROCKS?

Absolute ages

The Smithsonian National Museum of Natural History teaches:

> Rocks contain atomic clocks. They enable geologists to calculate when a rock formed—its absolute age—by measuring its radioactive elements. At last, geologists were able to attach years to the fossil-based, relative time scale and figure out, for example, exactly when the dinosaurs ruled the Earth. (www.mnh.si.edu/earth/text/3_1_2_3.html)

What the museum may not tell you is that not all rocks contain "atomic clocks." Instead, igneous (formerly molten) rocks and metamorphic rocks are the best candidates, while sedimentary rocks (which contain fossils) generally lack atomic clocks. There are many problems with this "absolute" method of age-dating rocks, and many assumptions involved with these methods. A major assumption of any radioisotope dating method is that the decay rate of a given isotope (an atomic nucleus with a given number of neutrons) is constant—that it has always been what it is today. Radioisotope methods can only be used to estimate a reliable age if nuclear decay rates have always been constant. After all, a clock would not give the correct time if it were to dramatically speed up or slow down. A group of scientists participating in the RATE (Radioisotopes and the Age of the Earth) project has recently uncovered several lines of evidence, which confirm that decay rates have not always been constant and were faster in the past:

- Measurements of helium diffusing (leaking) out of zircon crystals. The helium is produced by radioactive decay, but over time it can leak out of the crystals. If the zircons were billions of years old, there should be very little helium left since it would have had plenty of time to diffuse away, yet there is still a tremendous amount of helium in the zircons—consistent with an age of about 6,000 years.
- The detection of ^{14}C in coal and in diamonds. Since ^{14}C is a short-lived radioisotope, it cannot survive for millions of years. This is compelling evidence that these diamonds and coal deposits are thousands of years old at most. Additionally, ^{14}C is found in essentially all fossil organic material throughout the geologic column.

The RATE researchers suggest that the accelerated decay happened at two different times in earth's history—during the initial creation event, and during the Flood. For more information, see D. DeYoung, *Thousands ... Not Billions,* Institute for Creation Research, 2005, and visit www.answersingenesis.org/go/dating.

Most of the rock layers found around the world were laid down during the year-long Flood of Noah's day.

HOW OLD ARE ROCKS?

Relative ages

Relative ages are assigned to rocks based on the idea that the layers that are lower in the strata were deposited before rock layers that are higher. This is known as the Law of Superposition and can be applied to layers that are found in one location and are continuous; however, it cannot easily be applied across the board to layers found scattered around the world.

A relative age is an age that is based on a comparison with another rock. This is in contrast to "absolute" ages, which are based on direct age-dating of rocks (through radioisotope methods, for example).

Of course, the time associated with the layering of rocks is much smaller than the museum exhibits tell you—most fossil-bearing sedimentary rocks were probably laid down during the Flood over a period of days or months, not many millions of years.

UNCONFORMITIES—
MILLIONS OF YEARS OF
MISSING ROCK?

The American Museum of Natural History claims:

> Geologists' understanding of the Earth is in part based on the information gathered from exposed parts of the planet's crust, such as cliff faces, mountains, or canyons. These rocks reveal the history of the Earth, and enable scientists to piece it together. A classic example is the Hutton Unconformity where the rock outcrop is exposed at Siccar Point, Scotland. It was here in 1788 that James Hutton realized many geological truths that remain valid today.
>
> There, in a sea cliff, Hutton observed flat-lying layers of red sandstones resting on top of nearly vertical layers of gray shales. He realized that the gray shales, which had been deposited in water, must have been uplifted, tilted, eroded, and then once again submerged by an ocean from which the red sandstones were deposited. This so-called "unconformity" represents an extensive period during which no sediments were deposited—20 million years in the case of the Hutton Unconformity. This discovery overturned previous beliefs that the Earth was only 4,000 years old, and spawned the field of modern geoscience. (www.amnh.org/rose/hope/rocks/)

Notice that the "overturning" of the biblical timeframe (a 6,000 year-old earth, not 4,000 years old) was based on Hutton's *interpretations* of what he saw. What he observed were layers of rock on top of each other; what he *interpreted* was that millions of years occurred between the deposition of these layers. However, it stretches the imagination to think that, in this example, 20 million years passed without any sediments being deposited or eroded.

Dr. Ariel Roth, former director of the Geoscience Research Institute of Loma Linda, California, wrote:

> The difficulty with the extended time proposed for these gaps is that one cannot have deposition, nor can one have much erosion. With deposition, there is no gap, because sedimentation continues. With erosion, one would expect abundant channeling and the formation of deep gullies, canyons and valleys; yet, the contacts are usually "nearly planar." Over the long periods of time envisaged for these processes, erosion would erode the underlying layers and much more. ("Those gaps in the sedimentary layers," *Origins*, vol. 15, 1988, p. 90.)

Dr. Andrew Snelling explains unconformities this way:

Where erosion can clearly be seen to have occurred at these breaks between rock strata ..., creationists maintain that the erosion was very rapid, facilitated in many cases by erosion occurring in soft, "non-hardened" rock. Consequently, rather than having a land surface exposed for enormous periods of time after an ocean retreated, the same Flood processes responsible for depositing the sedimentary layers were also capable of eroding significant thicknesses of both loose sediment and consolidated rock. ("The case of the "missing" geologic time," *Creation* **14**:3,1992, pp. 30–35, online at www.answersingenesis.org/creation/v14/i3/time.asp.)

Dinosaur fossils, such as this one, are several thousand years old, at most.

FOSSIL EXHIBITS

Fossils of strange creatures, such as this trilobite, are remnants of creatures that lived before the Flood.

IS THERE AN ORDER TO THE FOSSIL RECORD?

In most museums, you'll find an illustration of the fossil record, showing Precambrian fossil layers at the bottom and Cenozoic layers toward the top. According to evolutionary history, these layers represent snapshots of the evolutionary process over millions of years.

However, creationists have a different interpretation. Based on what the Bible says, some creationists expect the fossil record to be divided into two broad categories. One category, a mix of plants and animals, would include many strange creatures from a world that was destroyed by the Flood. Above it would be a familiar mix of plants and animals from the world after the Flood.

But what could explain the progression of layers laid down *during* the Flood (first category mentioned above)?

One possibility is that the order reflects the sequence that the Flood buried different environments, beginning at the ocean floor. Genesis indicates that the Flood began with a violent breakup of the ocean floor. If so, it makes sense that sea creatures were buried before land animals.

Within this model, as the floodwaters rose over the coast, they swept away organisms on the shore, then farther and farther inland, with each new surge destroying another ecosystem. In this way, organisms could be buried based on the geographic and ecological order in which the floodwaters overwhelmed them.

Within this model, the upper portion of the fossil record, which contains a more familiar mix of organisms, is from the world *after* the Flood. Harvard-trained paleontologist Dr. Kurt Wise states:

> When the upper portion of the fossil record was first described, it was described by percent of fossils in a given layer that were modern species. At the bottom, few species modern, and then increasing in modern-ness as you go up.

This sequence is consistent with what the Bible says. After the Flood, each kind of organism quickly diversified and spread across the surface of the earth. Many of these creatures appear to have been buried during a series of smaller catastrophes in the unstable world following the Flood.

There was much volcanic activity during the initial stages of the Flood.
This probably continued throughout the duration of the Deluge.

DIFFERENT TIME PERIODS OR ECOSYSTEMS?

The usual story behind the fossil record is that each layer represents a period in time during which certain animals lived and died. Again, creationists offer a different interpretation of the evidence. The following model, developed by Dr. Kurt Wise, presents one idea about how the fossil layers may have been deposited. (Note: although we use the given names for the various layers of the geologic column, we reject the long timescales associated with those names.)

4004 BC: The **Precambrian** strata represent earth's "basement rocks" that God formed during the initial creation period. The initial continent was distributed as is pictured by the Rodinia concept. Much of this initial continent was covered by shallow seas. Located along the edge of the continent, were hot water reefs. Massive floating forests existed. Further inland were the habitats of the original created kinds of animals and humans.

2349 BC: The Flood begins. The **Paleozoic** invertebrate animals that lived in the shallow seas were among the first to be covered with sediment. The sand dunes along Rodinia's beaches and coastal animals were carried out to sea and redeposited by floodwaters as the **Permo-Triassic** sands of the world.

The **Ediacaran** through **Cretaceous** layers largely represent how the Flood picked off, in sequence, the hot spring reefs (**Vendian/Cambrian** layers), the shallow seas (**Ordovician/Silurian** layers), the floating forest (*Sigillaria*/**Devonian/Mississippian/Pennsylvanian layers**), and finally the dinosaurs (**Triassic/ Jurassic/Cretaceous** layers). Land animals were among the last to be buried.

2300–2000 BC: The **Paleogene** and **Neogene** *(Tertiary and Quaternary)* were produced in the first couple centuries following the Flood.

For more information, see K. Wise, "The Hydrothermal Biome: a Pre-Flood Environment," *Proceedings of the Fifth International Conference on Creationism.* Creation Science Fellowhip, 2003, pp. 359–370.

Although there is some disagreement among creationist geologists about the sequence of events given here, most accept this model of fossil layer formation. They agree that, rather than representing time periods separated by millions of years, the rock and fossil layers are more accurately described as buried ecosystems.

This dinosaur fossil is not millions of years old!

HOW OLD ARE THE FOSSILS?

In museum fossil exhibits, you'll often see statements such as, "This fossil is 65 million years old." How are these ages determined?

Fossils themselves are not usually directly dated. They are not found with tags that indicate their age. Instead, rock layers that contain supposed datable igneous (volcanic and plutonic) rocks above or below a fossil are used to estimate the age of the fossil. The age of the fossil is based on the range of ages assigned to the layers above and below it. However, as we've seen elsewhere ("How old are the rocks?"), many assumptions are involved in dating rock layers using radioisotope methods. Research has shown that the millions or billions of years results are not reliable.

"Index fossils" are also used to assign ages to some rock layers. This method assumes that the distribution of index fossils and the correlation of strata are well understood on a global scale. Where do the ages of index fossils come from? Again, the ages are based on many assumptions about past events and have been shown to be unreliable.

So how old are the fossils? Most are the remains of the global Flood 4,300 years ago. Some are from the Ice Age, while others are from localized post-Flood catastrophes.

Creationist geologists and paleontologists continue to debate which fossil layers are from the Flood and which formed later. They are working on presenting a cohesive model of the fossil record. However, we can say for certain that the fossils are at *most* thousands of years old—not millions.

Many specimens featured throughout museums are based on fossilized bones, not actual living examples.

WHAT CAN WE LEARN FROM FOSSILS?

Many of the more ancient animal specimens featured throughout museums are based on fossilized bones. As you examine the creatures, think about which parts of the display are actually based on the fossils and which are interpretations.

For example, can we really know the exact diet of an animal based on its tooth structure? Can we know where it lived? How it moved? What color it was? Whether it was warm-blooded or cold-blooded? How it interacted with other animals? When it lived? When and how it died?

Ice cores can be used as an age-gauge; however they need to be properly interpreted.

ICE AGE EXHIBITS

The extinction of the woolly mammoth remains a mystery to most museum curators.

THOSE WILD AND WOOLLY MAMMOTHS

The extinction of the woolly mammoth, and many other Ice Age mammals, is presented as a mystery in most museums. However, meteorologist Michael Oard offers a plausible explanation for the disappearance of the mammoths, based on his model of the post-Flood Ice Age in his book *Frozen in Time*. After the Ice Age ended (around 3,500 years ago), temperature differences between summer and winter would have become more extreme in the northern latitudes. The animals would have needed to quickly adjust to much colder winters. Oard explains how this affected the mammoths and other animals that lived in these areas (e.g., Siberia, Alaska, the Yukon, northern parts of the U.S.A.):

> They would have required extra food to keep themselves warm. In addition to suffering from the cold, the ice sheets were melting and causing occasional superfloods. They also had to contend with gigantic dust storms, boggy ground from permafrost at the edge of the ice sheets, drought, grass fires, etc. The woolly mammoth and other large herbivores would be especially hard hit, partly because they required so much more food and water. They would be tottering on the edge of extinction within a short time. Carnivores and carrion birds would have their fill for a time, but as their food source died, it would be their turn to go extinct. The end–Ice Age mass extinctions were selective in that mainly large animals went extinct. (*Frozen in Time*, Master Books, 2004, chapter available at www.answersingenesis.org/home/area/fit/chapter16.asp.)

Oard suggests that the main cause of Ice-Age-animal extinction in the Northern Hemisphere was giant dust storms that resulted from a drying climate and changing temperatures. He bases his ideas on the fact that most of the mammoths and other animals are found entombed in wind-blown silt (Loess).

> Loess is rather common south of and within the periphery of the former ice sheets in the Northern Hemisphere. It forms a thick blanket in parts of central China. This was probably desert loess that blew in from the west. ... large parts of Siberia are also covered with a layer of loess. In North America, we find large areas of stabilized sand dunes; for instance, extensive sand dunes cover areas of the Great Plains. The Nebraska sand hills blanket a large portion of western Nebraska and are up to 400 feet deep! Similar dunes are found north of the Cypress Hills in southeast Alberta and southwest Saskatchewan. Dunes are common in northern Europe and northwest Asia. Today, all of these dunes are mostly stabilized by vegetation. The dunes attest to the severity of the drought and dust storms during deglaciation. (*Frozen in Time*, Master Books, 2004, chapter available at www. answersingenesis.org/home/area/fit/chapter16.asp.)

Does ice buildup actually reflect annual layers?

HOW TO READ AN ICE CORE

Most ice cores are alleged to show hundreds of thousands of annual layers.

However, meteorologist Michael Oard points out that precipitation levels were much greater during the post-Flood Ice Age, resulting in a number of the core's lower layers being built up annually. While he agrees that annual layers are discernible in the upper layers, he suggests that the lower layers do not represent individual annual layers.

> ... the uniformitarian and creationist estimates of annual thickness are much the same at the top of the Greenland ice sheet. The difference between the two models becomes more and more significant deeper in the ice core. Because of extreme annual layer thinning at the bottom of the core in the uniformitarian model compared to the creationist model, the uniformitarian scientists may be counting 100 layers that they think are annual. These layers in the creationist model may represent only one year. So, the uniformitarian scientists in actuality would be counting storm layers or other cycles of weather that can often duplicate the annual cycle. For instance, a storm has a warm and cold sector with different measurements of the variables, producing a cycle in the variables. These storm oscillations may be on the order of several days. Even the uniformitarian scientists recognize that storms and other phenomena, like moving snow dunes, may result in the counting of an annual cycle, ... (*Frozen in Time*, Master Books, 2004, chapter available online at www.answersingenesis. org/home/area/fit/chapter12.asp.)

Crude oils themselves do not take long to be generated from appropriate organic matter.

COAL AND OIL EXHIBITS

Coal and oil were formed over a short time period during and after the Flood.

HOW WAS COAL AND OIL FORMED?

Concerning the formation of oil, geologist Dr. Andrew Snelling states:

Crude oils themselves do not take long to be generated from appropriate organic matter. Most petroleum geologists believe crude oils form mostly from plant material, such as diatoms (single-celled marine and freshwater photosynthetic organisms) and beds of coal (huge fossilized masses of plant debris). The latter is believed to be the source of most Australian crude oils and natural gas because coal beds are in the same sequences of sedimentary rock layers as the petroleum reservoir rocks.

Thus, for example, it has been demonstrated in the laboratory that moderate heating of the brown coals of the Gippsland Basin of Victoria, Australia, to simulate their rapid deeper burial, will generate crude oil and natural gas similar to that found in reservoir rocks offshore in only 2–5 days.

All the available evidence points to a recent catastrophic origin for the world's vast oil deposits, from plant and other organic debris, consistent with the biblical account of earth history.

Vast forests grew on land and water surfaces in the pre-Flood world, and the oceans teemed with diatoms and other tiny photosynthetic organisms. Then during the global Flood cataclysm, the forests were uprooted and swept away. Huge masses of plant debris were rapidly buried in what thus became coal beds, and organic matter generally was dispersed throughout the many catastrophically deposited sedimentary rock layers.

The coal beds and fossiliferous sediment layers became deeply buried as the Flood progressed. As a result, the temperatures in them increased sufficiently to rapidly generate crude oils and natural gas from the organic matter in them. These subsequently migrated until they were trapped in reservoir rocks and structures, thus accumulating to form today's oil and gas deposits. ("The Origin of Oil," *Answers* **2**:1, 2007, pp. 74–77, online at www.answersingenesis.org/articles/am/v2/n1/origin-of-oil.)

Most museums teach that cave formations take hundreds of thousands of years to form. However, through photo monitoring, some have been observed to grow several inches in just a few days!

CAVE EXHIBITS

Cave formations such as these don't need hundreds of thousands of years to form.

HOW WERE CAVES FORMED?

After the original rock layers were deposited during the Flood event, hot waters rising from deeper inside the earth quickly enlarged cracks and conduits through the sedimentary layers, leaving behind vast passages and chambers. Later, water seeping from the surface continued to shape the underground world, forming the many and varied beautiful formations—stalactites, stalagmites, etc.

Most museums teach that cave formations take hundreds of thousands of years to form. However, through photo monitoring, some have been observed to grow several inches in just a few days!

For more information, visit www.answersingenesis.org/go/caves.

Many gems and minerals formed from processes acting on the mineral-rich sediments in the Flood.

GEM AND MINERAL EXHIBITS

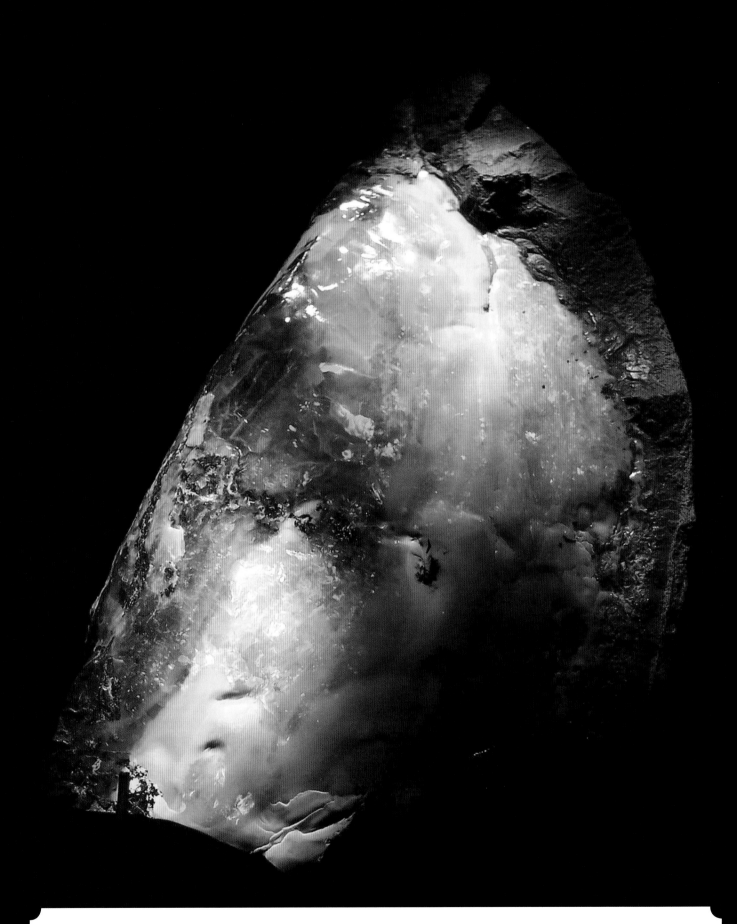

Len Cram has found that opal formation over millions of years is a myth—he has created opals in a matter of months!

OPALS

A Bible-believing scientist in Australia has dedicated his life to researching the formation of opals. Len Cram has found that the millions-of-years story is a myth. In fact, he has created high quality opals in his laboratory in a matter of months!

All it takes is an electrolyte (a chemical solution that is electrically charged), a source of silica and water, and some alumina and feldspar.

The opal-forming process is one of ion exchange, a chemical process that involves building the opal structure ion by ion (an ion is an electrically charged atom, or group of atoms [molecule]). ... The ion exchange process starts at some point and spreads until all the critical ingredients, in this case the electrolyte, are used up. This initial formation process takes place quickly, in a matter of months, in Len's laboratory.

After the initial formation in a matter of weeks, the opal has beautiful colour patterns, but it still has a lot of water in it. Slowly over months, further chemical changes take place which consolidate the silica gel. These changes create varying patterns of colour and "squeeze" the water out. It is not the initial forming that takes time; rather, it is this restructuring. Only after the opal has restructured is it stable and useful as a gemstone.

Based on this research, Dr. Andrew Snelling explains how natural opals have formed:

At some point in the host rock [which formed during the Flood], the correct mixture of electrolyte and other ingredients is present. The chemical process starts and expands outward. It transforms the host sandstone or opal dirt into precious opal through the ion exchange process. As it does, it uses up the electrolyte. When it is all used up, the process stops and no more precious opal forms. After this initial formation, the silica gel naturally restructures, becoming more compact, "squeezing" out water as it does.

(Growing opals—Australian style, *Creation* **12**:1, 1989, pp. 10–15, online at www.answersingenesis.org/creation/v12/i1/opals.asp.)

Carbon-14 atoms in diamonds provide strong evidence for a limited earth age of just thousands of years.

DIAMONDS

The Hope diamond, and its billion-year-old history, is featured in the Smithsonian Museum of Natural History.

Dr. John Baumgardner has conducted research on diamonds which shows that these gems cannot be billions of years old:

> Twelve diamond samples were obtained and prepared for ^{14}C analysis. Such measurements had not been previously reported because diamonds are assumed to be at least a billion years old and therefore entirely free of ^{14}C. ... carbon-14 atoms were found in every diamond tested. The conclusion is clear: carbon-14 atoms in coal, diamonds, and a host of other materials provide strong evidence for a limited earth age of just thousands of years. The pervasive presence of carbon-14 in earth materials supports biblical creation. (D. DeYoung, "Raising the Bar on Creation Research," *Answers* **1**:1, 2006, pp. 22–24, online at www.answersingenesis.org/articles/am/v1/n1/creation-research.)

Dr. Andrew Snelling explains the formation of diamonds this way:

> Today's diamond deposits at today's land surface are in kimberlite and lamproite pipes that were intruded through strata most of which were undoubtedly deposited by the Flood. This means that the rapid ascent of molten kimberlites and lamproites and the explosive volcanism that resulted in the pipes must have occurred late in the Flood, soon after it, or sometime later .... (Diamonds—evidence of explosive geological processes, *Creation* **16**:1(1993), pp. 42–45, online at www.answersingenesis. org/creation/v16/i1/diamonds.asp.)

"The heavens declare the glory of God; And the firmament shows His handiwork." Psalm 19:1

HALL OF OUR EXPANSIVE UNIVERSE

The heavens declare the glory of God; And the firmament shows His handiwork (Psalm 19:1).

God created the sun to give light on the earth during the day, the moon to shed light during the night, and the rest of the heavenly bodies to mark the seasons and signs. All of the many billions of galaxies, each containing many billions of stars were created instantaneously as the infinite Creator spoke them into existence on the fourth day of that first week, 6,000 years ago.

This section of the guide provides answers to the naturalistic explanation of our expansive universe.

How many of these stars are orbited by planets? Scientists continue to study the answer to this question.

EXTRASOLAR PLANETS?

Astronomers have discovered extrasolar planets that orbit distant stars. Although most of these planets have not been directly observed, they have been detected indirectly—usually by the gravitational "tug" they produce on the star they orbit. The principles being used here are operational science, so we have good reason to believe that these are indeed real planets that God created on Day 4 of the Creation Week 6,000 years ago.

According to astrophysicist Dr. Jason Lisle, these extrasolar planets are actually a problem for naturalistic ideas about the origin of the universe. Secular astronomers had expected that other solar systems would resemble ours—with small planets forming very close to their star, and large planets forming far away. But many of these extrasolar planets are just the opposite; they are large Jupiter-sized planets orbiting very close to their star.

This is inconsistent with evolutionary models of solar system formation, but it's not a problem for biblical creation. God can create many different varieties of solar systems, and apparently He has done just that.

For more information, visit www.answersingenesis.org/docs2005/0420extrasolar_planets.asp and www. answersingenesis.org/tj/v17/i1/solar_system.asp.

Comets are made of dust and water in the form of ice.

IS THERE LIQUID WATER ELSEWHERE IN THE UNIVERSE?

Physicist Dr. Russell Humphreys believes that the Genesis account of creation implies that there was a water origin for our universe.

Water (often as ice) is everywhere in the solar system: in comets, planetary rings, on moons of the large planets, possibly on the asteroid Ceres and at the poles of the Earth's moon, formerly on Venus, presently on Earth and deep in its rocky mantle, and in the polar caps of Mars. Water, as falling chunks of ice, may have pounded out many of the craters we see everywhere in the solar system.

He believes that Martian water may have come from space and from the interior of Mars.

Many creation scientists have suspected that the Genesis Flood was a catastrophe which affected the whole solar system, not just the Earth. If high-velocity chunks of ice made the craters on Mars, the ice would turn to water vapor upon impact. The very large Martian volcanoes (Mons Olympus, etc.) would have belched out huge volumes of water vapor (even the smaller volcanoes of Earth do that).

Dr. Humphreys believes that the water may have evaporated into space, combined with minerals on the surface of Mars, or soaked into the ground becoming permafrost.

(R. Humphreys, "Water on Mars: A Creationist Response," www.answersingenesis.org/docs/203.asp.)

God created the moon and other heavenly bodies to support life on earth.

DOES WATER = LIFE?

Life as we know it depends on water. Scientists who accept evolutionary naturalism believe that if they find water, they will eventually find life. However, the existence of water elsewhere does not automatically translate into the existence of intelligent life outside of planet earth.

In fact, as we've seen elsewhere in this guide, it takes much more than liquid water for life to originate. And after 40 years of searching the skies for signs of life, not one real live alien has been found. Scientists have also found that there are many features that set the earth apart from other planets, and help us know that God created it to be inhabited (Isaiah 45:18).

Biblically, it doesn't seem possible that life exists outside of our planet for the following reasons:

* The Bible does not mention space alien life forms. If extra-terrestrials *did* exist, we might expect the Bible to reveal something about them, or tell us to expect a visit from them someday.
* God placed a curse on the entire universe after Adam sinned. So if there *were* other beings out there, they would also be suffering from the effects of *our* sin. Additionally, when Jesus came to earth, He came as a man. Jesus didn't become an alien. And He remains forever the God-man Jesus Christ.
* God created the sun, moon, stars, and other planets with special purposes (Genesis 1:14–15). God designed the heavenly bodies to support life on earth. The earth has a very special place in the universe.
* The whole of the Bible is centered on how God has dealt with humans since the beginning. Jesus became a man and came to earth to die for the sin of mankind (1 Corinthians 15:1–4), not for a race of alien beings. He is preparing a place in Heaven for His children, not a race of extraterrestrials.

For more information, visit www.answersingenesis.org/home/area/faq/alien.asp.

"Big bang cosmology has become a bandwagon of thought that reflects faith as much as objective truth."

WHAT ABOUT THE BIG BANG?

The most popular naturalistic explanation about the origin of the universe is the big bang hypothesis. At its simplest, this view suggests that the universe emerged rapidly from a hot, dense state several billion years ago. However, there are differing versions of the big bang idea, with disagreement among the versions. As one scientist has pointed out, there are many problems with this view:

> Big bang cosmology is probably as widely believed as has been any theory of the universe in the history of Western civilization. It rests, however, on many untested, and in some cases untestable, assumptions. Indeed, big bang cosmology has become a bandwagon of thought that reflects faith as much as objective truth. (G. Burbidge, "Why only one big bang?" *Scientific American* **266**:2, 1992, p. 96)

There are many biblical and scientific problems with the big bang hypothesis. A few examples follow.

- The Beginning: The big bang teaches that the sun came first, and then the earth. However, the Bible teaches that God created the earth first, and then the sun (Genesis 1).
- The End: The big bang teaches that in the distant future, in accord with the Second Law of Thermodynamics, all the energy in the universe will be evently distributed, and the temperature will be a fraction of a degree above absolute zero. However, the Bible teaches that the heavens will be destroyed by fire (2 Peter 3:10–12), and that God will create a new heavens and earth (2 Peter 3:13; Revelation 21:1). For more information, visit www.answersingenesis.org/creation/v25/i4/longage.asp.
- Light travel-time problem: The big bang requires that opposite regions of the visible universe must have exchanged energy by radiation, since these regions of space look the same in Cosmic Microwave Background (CMB) maps. But there has not been enough time for light to travel this distance. This remains a serious difficulty for big bang supporters, as evidenced by their many competing conjectures that attempt to solve it.

For more information, visit www.answersingenesis.org/creation/v25/i4/lighttravel.asp.
For more information, visit www.answersingenesis.org/go/astronomy.

Our solar system didn't form on its own millions of years ago; it was created by God 6,000 years ago.

WHAT ABOUT THE NEBULAR HYPOTHESIS?

In retelling how our solar system originated, many museums will feature the nebular hypothesis. This idea suggests that the solar system formed from a spinning cloud of dust and gasses which contracted and formed the sun and various planets.

There are many scientific and biblical problems with this idea:

- It is an inherently atheistic idea (it attempts to explain the origin of our solar system without supernatural causes).
- It contradicts the biblical order of events: God created the earth first, out of nothing, and then instantaneously created the heavenly bodies four days later.
- Not all planets in our solar system rotate in the same direction (Venus and Uranus rotate clockwise, while the other planets rotate counterclockwise).
- The laws of physics dictate that gas will expand in space, not contract.

For more information, visit www.answersingenesis.org/go/astronomy.

The Bible indicates that the universe has been "stretched out" or expanded.

IS THE UNIVERSE EXPANDING?

The Bible indicates in several places that the universe has been "stretched out" or expanded (see below for a brief list). For example, the prophet Isaiah taught that God stretches out the heavens like a curtain and spreads them out like a tent to dwell in (Isaiah 40:22). This would suggest that the universe has actually increased in size since its creation. God is stretching it out, causing it to expand. Secular scientists once believed that the universe was eternal and unchanging. However, most astronomers today believe that the universe is indeed expanding. In the 1920s, astronomers discovered that virtually all clusters of galaxies appear to be moving away from all other clusters; this indicates that the entire universe is expanding.

Psalm 104:2:

> Who cover Yourself with light as with a garment,
> Who stretch out the heavens like a curtain.

Isaiah 42:5:

> Thus says God the LORD,
> Who created the heavens and stretched them out,
> Who spread forth the earth and that which comes from it,
> Who gives breath to the people on it,
> And spirit to those who walk on it:

Isaiah 44:24:

> Thus says the LORD, your Redeemer,
> And He who formed you from the womb:
> " I am the LORD, who makes all things,
> Who stretches out the heavens all alone,
> Who spreads abroad the earth by Myself;"

Jeremiah 10:12:

> He has made the earth by His power,
> He has established the world by His wisdom,
> And has stretched out the heavens at His discretion.

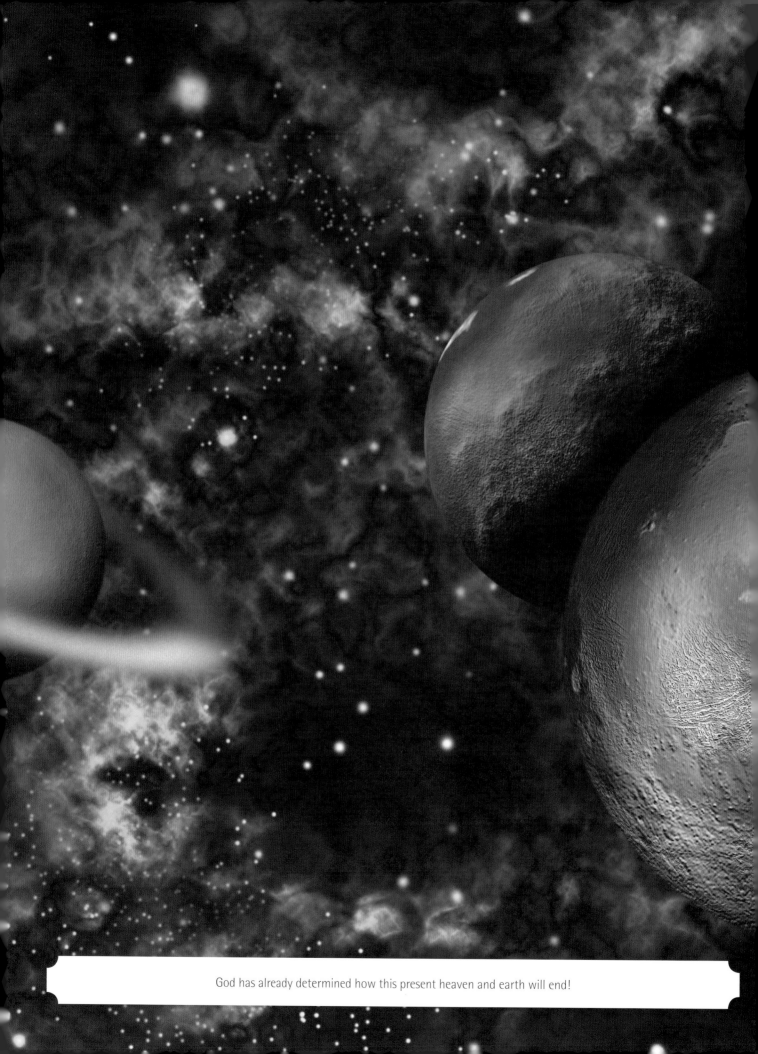

God has already determined how this present heaven and earth will end!

WHAT IS THE FATE OF OUR UNIVERSE?

There are many different naturalistic ideas about how the universe will come to an end. The most common is a prediction of the big bang idea. Robert Matthews, science correspondent for *The Sunday Telegraph*, puts it this way:

> A mere thousand billion years from now, all the stars will have used up their fuel and fizzled out. There will still be occasional flashes in the perpetual night: the death throes of stars so large that they have collapsed in on themselves to form black holes. Even these will eventually evaporate in a blast of radiation. For the next 10^{122} years, this Hawking radiation will be the only show in town. By then, even the most massive black holes will evaporate, leaving the universe with nothing to do for an unimaginable 10^{26} years. ... In the beginning, there may have been light, but in the end, it seems, there will be nothing but darkness. (R. Matthews, "To infinity and beyond," *New Scientist* **158**:2129, April 11, 1998, pp. 27–30.)

This view contradicts the biblical teaching that God will destroy the present heavens with fire, and will create a new heavens and earth for His children (2 Peter 3:13; Revelation 21:1). Those who have received the free gift of eternal life can rest in the salvation given by God, and His promise of spending eternity with Him. God is sovereignly in control of His creation and nothing happens apart from what He has decreed. He has already determined how this present heaven and earth will end: rather than beginning with a big bang, the universe will end with one!

2 Peter 3:7–13:
But the heavens and the earth which are now preserved by the same word, are reserved for fire until the day of judgment and perdition of ungodly men. But, beloved, do not forget this one thing, that with the Lord one day is as a thousand years, and a thousand years as one day. The Lord is not slack concerning His promise, as some count slackness, but is longsuffering toward us, not willing that any should perish but that all should come to repentance. But the day of the Lord will come as a thief in the night, in which the heavens will pass away with a great noise, and the elements will melt with fervent heat; both the earth and the works that are in it will be burned up. Therefore, since all these things will be dissolved, what manner of persons ought you to be in holy conduct and godliness, looking for and hastening the coming of the day of God, because of which the heavens will be dissolved, being on fire, and the elements will melt with fervent heat? Nevertheless we, according to His promise, look for new heavens and a new earth in which righteousness dwells.

We were not made out of the elements that were produced inside stars!

ARE WE STARSTUFF?

Some universe-oriented exhibits may claim that "we are all starstuff." That is, the elements that we are made of were produced inside stars that formed after the big bang.

However, there are many problems with the idea that stars formed from the big bang. Notice the conjecture in this frank admission by the editors of *Astronomy* magazine:

> Astronomers don't know for sure how the universe made its first stars, but they do have a reasonably good guess. (As you can imagine, there's no way to observe the formation of the first generation of stars, so all the work is based upon theoretical considerations.) The best scenario has molecular hydrogen playing the role of the cooling agent. If the clouds from which stars formed were some four to five times denser in the early universe than they are today, then enough collisions between hydrogen atoms would have taken place to create a lot of molecular hydrogen. The big question is: Were the first galaxies that much denser? Obviously the overall density of the universe was much higher back in the early days, but no one knows whether the star-forming clouds were this much denser.

Most astronomers would say that the fact that stars do exist tells us that the density was higher back then, because otherwise there would be no stars ... Nowadays, of course, nature has found a simpler, easier way to cool the clouds (with water), so that's what she uses. ("Talking Back, Water, water (almost) everywhere," *Astronomy* 27:6, 1999, p. 16)

Scientists have not observed the formation of stars, but have observed them changing brightness and exploding.

DO STARS EVOLVE?

Stars change to some extent, but not over billions of years. Some stars spontaneously change brightness. Others explode. These are things that scientists have been able to observe. However, scientists do not observe star formation, nor the secular stellar evolution cycle that is taught in so many textbooks and museums.

Some of what astronomers describe as "stellar evolution" does take place. However, the process is misnamed, and parts of it are questionable. According to this theory, the life of a star is said to begin with the collapse of a gas cloud-a doubtful beginning. Bypassing this fundamental origin problem, a young star is said to begin in the "main sequence" category. These are average stars with a stable light output. The great majority of stars are in the main sequence, including our sun. When a star's hydrogen fuel runs low, it becomes a red giant or super-giant star. Such a star has expanded hundreds of times in size and has become somewhat cooler. Red giants include Betelgeuse and Aldebaran.

Next, the star may either explode as a supernova or may slowly collapse into a small, hot white dwarf star. The companion star circling Sirius is such a dwarf. Such stars are said to be very old.

Notice that the entire life of a star is an aging process: main sequence-red giant-white dwarf. Instead of stellar evolution, it might better be called stellar decay, degradation, or degeneration. Computer studies conclude that each stage of a star lasts for millions or billions of years (depending on the star's mass), but in the recent-creation view, there has not been enough time for such change. And some observed star changes appear to be much more rapid than computer models suggest! For example, there is evidence that the dwarf companion of Sirius formed from a red giant in just 1,000 years. Other stars have also shown unexpected color changes, indicating that the aging process of some stars may be much more rapid than generally believed. Most stars have probably not changed substantially in appearance since the creation described in Genesis. The sun has certainly remained as a faithful "main sequence" star from the beginning. Since all the stars were made on the fourth day (Gen. 1:16–19), they are all actually the same age. From the beginning they have differed from each other in color and brightness— "in splendor" (1 Cor. 15:41).

INDEX